FULL

A Memoir of Overcoming
an Eating Disorder

SARA GOTTFRIED

First paperback edition February 2022

Book design by Shelby Gates
Edited by Christine Meade

ISBN: 978-0-578-36224-3

Published by KDP Publishing
https://kdp.amazon.com/en_US/

TABLE *of* CONTENTS

FORWARD

From the first time I met Sara on a warm spring day, I knew she had a spark. She embodied the qualities of a fighter—strong, determined, and confident. Her ability to navigate challenges and personal hardships had not diminished her spirit but rather empowered her.

Sara's memoir, *Full: A Memoir of Overcoming an Eating Disorder*, provides a raw look into her journey with an eating disorder. Readers will not only learn about Sara's story but will feel empowered and inspired to overcome their own struggles with disordered eating. I believe that Sara's story gives readers the confidence they need to share their own battles.

As I write this foreword for her inspiring memoir, I share words that I always knew but have been reaffirmed in Sara's memoir: be kind to yourself, you can overcome your own challenges, it's okay to fall, get back up and keep fighting. You have the power!

—MICHAEL J. DE PONS

PROLOGUE

February 22, 2015

Dear Future Sara,

When I am recovered, I will be a top social worker in Los Angeles, California. I will help families and children find stable jobs, adequate housing, and consistent food. I will work during the day and practice yoga at night. I hope to be a certified yoga teacher. Some days, I will do yoga, others I will hit the gym or maybe take a stroll through the canyons with my dog. I hope to be married or have a partner who I can lean on. I picture myself going to the scrapbooking store. I will be in control of my thoughts. I will be able to enjoy a party or a spontaneous ice cream trip. I won't feel so isolated and alone. I will be able to wear skinny jeans. Clothes won't be so baggy on me, and shopping will be more enjoyable. I will be able to look in the mirror and say, "Damn girl, you look good!" When I look in the mirror, I will see Sara, not Eating Disorder Sara. I hope to share my story. I hope to read this journal entry and know that it is a thing of the past.

Yours Truly,
Sara

Chapter One

"We started out as ultrasensitive truth tellers. We saw everyone around us smiling and repeating "I'm fine! I'm fine! I'm fine!" and we found ourselves unable to join them in all the pretending. We had to tell the truth, which was: "Actually, I'm not fine." But no one knew how to handle hearing that truth, so we found other ways to tell it. We used whatever else we could find—drugs, booze, food, money, our arms, our bodies. We acted out our truth instead of speaking it and everything became a godforsaken mess. But we were just trying to be honest."

—GLENNON DOYLE

November 2012

I sat on a vinyl chair in the waiting room of the doctor's office. It was my yearly physical. I was sixteen years old. The bitter smell mixed with a soapy undertone permeated the waiting room. Across from me, children played with germ-infested toys as mothers held tissues hostage to clean up the ever-dripping mucus. I felt nervous. I always felt nervous going to the doctor's office. It was an experience filled with needles, endless questions, and long waits.

I noticed my foot shaking, as my hands lay underneath my thighs, making sweat handprints on the chair. It was a gloomy day outside, the sun hiding behind a thick layer of clouds. I was tempted to skim through the magazines on the table next to me, but I caught myself, as though a piece of yellow caution tape set down in front of me. *Sara, how many people have touched those?* It was an internal dialogue I had with myself at every doctor's appointment. That voice in the back of my head saying, *Don't put your face against that window, too many germs are on it. Don't touch the doorknob with your bare hand, too many snotty children have touched it. Be careful where you sit, who knows when they cleaned the chairs.* I was by no means a self-proclaimed germaphobe, but I was not one who enjoyed getting sick. Just as I took out my phone to play Solitaire, I heard my name. "Sara Gottfried!" I felt my body jump up fast, but my mind was still looking around for the nurse. *Here goes nothing.*

I followed the nurse in her pink-themed scrubs to the back office. We walked down a hall with floor-to-ceiling windows. The thin, faded carpet felt hard. Each step I took was followed by a creak in the floor. The air got mustier. I could feel my nostrils perk up as my body tried to decipher why the doctor's office smelled so bad. As I followed the nurse, she did not say anything. When a baby or a toddler has a physical, they are treated with so many *oohs and aahs*, cascades of smiles, and warmth. But after you have surpassed the cuteness stage, all the tender smiles and empathetic nods are replaced with a demeanor of, *You know the drill. Let's get this over with. I've already dealt with enough crying babies for today.*

As we passed by the nurse's station, she took me into a small room and prompted me to sit down. Once seated, I placed my forehead against the cold metal bar of the vision test machine. "I am going to display a series of letters. They will get smaller and smaller. Read through each row and if you cannot read a letter, just skip it," the nurse instructed. Her tone of voice was shallow, and her affect was flat.

Let me show this nurse how it is done. I read each letter, line by line and I aced it, per usual.

After the vision test, the nurse prepared to check my iron. I hated needles, and I hated that they did the test in the middle of the nurse's station, where there was lots of commotion. It was a sensory overload with metal trays of ready-to-go vaccines propped up in bins, medical supplies all over the place, and beeping sounds coming from every which direction. I sat on a black high-top stool, not even a chair, as the nurse asked me to hold out my right hand. She pinched the fleshy part of my middle finger and before she even counted to three, she prodded my finger with a needle. Good gracious, a countdown would have been nice. And just when I thought I was done being summoned around, she led me back into yet another room. I knew this was the last stop because it was the scale room. She checked my weight and measured my height. I did not think anything of it. It was the same old drill. They always checked my weight and height. I never really put too much thought into the number on the scale. It never seemed that accurate, as the nurse always fumbled around with the bar to get the scale even.

After my weight was checked, I followed the nurse into a private room, where I undressed, put on a paper hospital gown, and sat on the bed. Just as I was about to sneak a glimpse at the time on my phone, I heard a knock at the door. I quickly hid my phone underneath my thigh. My facial muscles tensed as my jaw locked in place, and my eyebrows furrowed. Dr. O'Brien walked into the room with her loud and boisterous smile. I gave her a brief nod with my signature eye roll and tried to swallow my annoyance. To describe Dr. O'Brien accurately is to describe one of the storytellers on a Disney World ride. She was so animated. Her presence was overwhelming. It was not necessarily the questions she asked, it was the way she asked them. She may have been a great doctor for young children but not for teenagers. Going to a physical at sixteen years old was already uncomfortable, why did she have to make it more uncomfortable?

"Hello, Sara! How are you today? It's great to see you!" said Dr. O'Brien.

I put on a fake smile and replied, "I'm good."

Dr. O'Brien proceeded to sit down and take vicarious notes, asking me a multitude of questions. Each questioned was answered by one simple word.

Dr. O'Brien: "How is school?"

Me: "Good."

Dr. O'Brien: "What is your favorite subject?"

Me: "English."

Dr. O'Brien: "That's awesome! Do you enjoy writing?"

Me: "Sometimes."

Dr. O'Brien: "How about activities? What after-school activities are you involved in?"

Me: "I do dance once a week and I did track last year."

Dr. O'Brien: "That's great! Are you going to do track this spring?"

Me: "I don't know."

Dr. O'Brien: "How about friends? Do you have a good group of friends?"

Me: "Yes."

Dr. O'Brien: "I like to hear that! Let's have you lay down on the bed."

Her ice-cold fingers felt around my stomach. It was uncomfortable. She pushed into my organs, asked me to take deep breaths in and out, and was so far in my personal space we might as well be sharing the same breath. Then she checked my ears, scratching my earlobes with the otoscope reminding me, yet again, that I had tubes in my ears. "Oh, Sara, your ears are so scratched up from the tubes you had as a child."

Thank you?

Next, she asked me to open wide and say, *Ahh,* so she could look at my tonsils. It felt like one invasion of my privacy after the next. "All right, Sara, you can sit up now, honey," said Dr. O'Brien.

Yes, finally, she is going to tell me I am all set, and I can leave. But instead of saying this, Dr. O'Brien sat down, typing up notes. Without even looking up at me, she said, "I think the weight you are at is a good weight to stay at."

My mind was so focused on wanting to get the hell of out there that her statement had no impact on me in the moment. Her suggestion went right over my head. At this point, I was not focused on my weight. I was sixteen years old. I weighed 115 pounds. I was 5'1". I never had weight issues. She had never commented on my weight prior to this appointment. I just smiled and nodded, hoping she would leave. And she did. We both did. But we each left not knowing the repercussions of that brief yet powerful statement.

Chapter Two

"We are all products of our environment; every person we meet, every new experience or adventure, every book we read, touches and changes us, making us the unique being we are."

—C.J. HECK

May 2013

Six months after my physical, I was one month out of finishing my sophomore year high school. I had a great year. I traveled to California with my dad where we rode in our yellow Camaro through the canyons to Solvang. I spent time on the Santa Monica Pier riding the famous Ferris wheel, and we transformed ourselves into children at Disneyland. That year I also celebrated my sweet sixteen at the Langham Hotel where my friends and I ate our way through the chocolate bar. I spent most of my Friday nights at Bertucci's with my friends, eating one too many rolls, glossing my lips with butter from the noodles of my favorite chicken picatta, and satisfying my sweet tooth with a good old fashioned five-dollar ice cream from Coldstone Creamery.

I was a good student. I put a lot of pressure on myself to do well. I was the type of student who did my homework immediately upon arriving home, stayed after school for help with math, and studied for tests weeks in advance. I color coded my classes with matching binders, pens, and highlighters, spent way too much money and time in Target and Staples re-stocking school supplies, and found lots of joy in using my agenda book. I was a quiet student who never wanted to be the obvious teacher's pet but strived to be liked by the teacher. My report cards usually revealed high honors with a steady grade point average.

During the spring of my sophomore year, I toiled around with the idea of joining the track team. I joined the winter and spring track team during my freshman year and enjoyed the social aspect. As for the running, well, I should probably take a moment to define running. Running, for me, looked more like skipping a few practices each week to go to Dunkin' Donuts with friends, hanging out in the locker room, or staying after to get a late pass for practice. Let's just say my name may have physically been on the roster, but I was not physically running much.

Although track would have been my golden ticket to get out of gym, I was not motivated enough to be on the team. Instead, I joined Workout World. It was a new gym that opened in the town over from me, and many of my friends had joined as well. There were the obvious gym rats there, buffed up on supplements who made it their full-time job to workout. There were the usual mothers trying to get thirty minutes of peace. Sometimes, I saw groups of teens working out, preparing for the next sports season. And then there was everyone else, like me, going for the simple act of working out because it made them feel good. I can recall looking around while on the elliptical, seeing muscular women with flat stomachs and sculped calves and thinking it would be nice to look that fit.

A week after joining, I felt that rush many Americans feel on New Year's Day when they click "confirm" on their computer screen to complete the 21 Day Fix Weight Loss Plan. I had this adrenaline rush of *Hey, I can do this. I can be healthy!* But what did "healthy" even mean? Like many, I thought a diet would be a quick, one-stop-shop solution. I mean, what's five pounds? It can't be too hard to lose five pounds, and if it makes me feel good about myself, then why not?

I came home from the gym one afternoon in late May, and my mom was standing over the stove, sautéing vegetables. The steam from the pan moisturized the microwave as she took out a bag of Uncle Ben's 90-second rice. I flicked my sneakers off, dumped my gym bag on the chair, sat down, and said, "Mom, I'm going on a diet."

My mom turned around and said, "I've been using this app, My Fitness Pal. You should use it, too."

I had been going to the gym for only a few weeks, but there was an immediate shift in my motivation after hearing my mom's response. I am not sure what type of response I was looking for in that moment. Perhaps, I was hoping she would say, "Sara, you don't need to go on a diet. You are perfectly fine the way you are." And even if she said that, would I have still pursued a diet? I don't know. Maybe. Regardless, her response intertwined with my determined personality was the confirmation I needed to go on a diet. And I did.

Perhaps my eagerness to diet stemmed from my childhood. Although I never had a weight problem or acted upon my thoughts related to body image, there were moments as a young girl when I wanted to change parts of my physical body. I never remember feeling or saying the word *fat*, but I felt physically different compared to everyone else. I was self-conscious, and I bought clothes in bigger sizes to hide my body. Sometimes, I zipped up sweatshirts to my chin, thinking somehow it made my body look smaller. I looked at mannequins, wishing I could adopt that body type. I never told anyone I felt this way. I never said any of these things out loud. These thoughts just floated around in my head. And maybe part of the reason I experienced these thoughts was because of my environment.

I grew up in a family with a hyper focus on food and appearance. My mom was no stranger to dieting. She engaged in the popular Hungry Girl and Weight Watchers phases, which ultimately meant I succumbed to both as well. The Hungry Girl phase led to low-calorie dinners that left me feeling hungrier than when I initially sat down. Recipes included Lasagna Cupcakes, hold the pasta, cue the wonton wrappers and Sloppy Jane Stir-Fry, hold all things carbs. Opening the snack drawer only led to increased hunger cues. There were boxes of 100-calorie Nabisco Oreo Crisps that tasted worse than the cardboard box they were packaged in and Skinny Cow chocolate turtles that were filled with plastic caramel. The freezer was equipped with Lean Cuisines. Supermarket trips often consisted of questions like, "Do we really need that?" and "Are you actually going to eat that?" Sometimes the mere act of putting in a bag of chips or freshly baked cookies led to, "Sara, are you on your period?" But it was not just my mom. There were other family members who glamorized unrealistic body ideals and allowed food and weight discourse to dominate family celebrations.

My dad was different. He never struggled with his weight or went on diets. Or if he did, I never noticed. He was the type of person people refer to as having a "fast metabolism." He can eat whatever he wants whenever he wants and not gain a single pound. He has an uncontrollable sweet tooth, which is his only food "problem." He's a big chocolate and ice cream guy; the type of person who throws a hissy fit if there is not any hot fudge in the house for his ice cream or if the candy jar is empty. So, it was not a shock to me that my mom was using a diet app. The real shock was that she never said, "Sara, you don't need to go on a diet," which is why my fingers typed, searched, and clicked away to download My Fitness Pal. From May to September 2013, I tracked my workouts and measured my food.

Breakfast: ½ tbsp. non-fat milk and 1 cup of Special K Strawberry Cereal

Lunch: 1 100-calorie 100% Whole Wheat Arnold Bread Sandwich Flat with 3 pieces of ham and 1 wedge of Original Laughing Cow Spreadable Cheese, 1 90-calorie Fiber One brownie, and a green apple

Dinner: 1 90-calorie Yoplait Light Yogurt with 2 tbsp. Original Vanilla Almond Bear Naked Granola, and berries

I didn't switch flavors, try different brands, or go off track in any way. My gym regimen consisted of an hour of the elliptical, treadmill, and bike daily. At the end of each day, I was consuming approximately 850 calories and burning 500 calories. And even on days when I had absolutely no energy to go to the gym, I dragged my butt there because it was easier to go than to have to deal with the anxiety-provoking thoughts of not going.

July 2013

Once July rolled around and I was on summer break, I joined my dad on bike rides, which averaged about twelve miles. Sometimes we biked along the Bourne Bridge in Cape Cod, which had become our summer tradition a few years prior. This summer was different, however, for me at least. Normally, we would eat lunch at a hole-in-the-wall seafood shack along the water, but now the thought of indulging in a greasy plate of crispy fried fish with French fries created distress. Instead, I packed my lunch. My usual lunch. And as I sat on the bench, chocolate sprinkles plastered to the table and dried up ketchup in the creases, I ate my tasteless sandwich, sick of ham and Laughing Cow cheese. Each bite felt like a gulp as I forced myself to swallow. What was once tasty, now became monotonous and boring. I could smell the seafood and the fishy aroma from my dad's fish n' chips, which triggered a flashback to the previous summer.

I remembered my dad and I sitting on a rickety picnic bench that looked slanted atop uneven gravel. Sitting across from one another, we shared a tin full of napkins, as we ate our way through pure yumminess. The paper plates looked as though they were going to rip apart from the grease of the fish n' chips. As I took my first bite, I broke apart the fish, crumbs flying. My fingers were instantly covered with grease as I crunched away at the crust. The fried fish was a delectable golden color. The French fries were seasoned with just the right amount of salt. There was no talking; not because there was not anything to say but because the food was that good. By the end, my lips were glossed over, my fingers needed more than a wet cloth, and my stomach was in heaven.

But during that summer of 2013, my motto became, *Any workout is better than no workout at all* and *What you eat in private you wear in public*, which meant fish n' chips and French fries had no room in my diet. And so, throughout the next five months, I rarely went out to eat. There were no summer nights filled with ice cream and s'mores. No fun in the sun. Going to the gym and eating the same three meals consumed my days. I did not hang out with friends because that meant there would be food. I kept to myself. I went to bed at seven p.m. every night, hoping to sleep off my grumbling stomach and hunger pains. Each morning, I was up at the crack of dawn, not because I was a true morning person, but because I was hungry. Actually, no, not hungry, more like starving. What started as wanting to lose a few pounds quickly spiraled. I weighed myself every day, and each week the number kept going down. I began to see how easy it was to get the weight off, which only fueled my adrenaline rush each time I stepped off the scale. If it was that easy to lose five pounds, what was another five? And another? And another?

It was not until August of that summer that things started to really change. We took a family trip to Burlington, Vermont, for a college tour at the University of Vermont. I wanted to study nutrition and become a dietician. Some may say this passion for weight loss perpetuated my desire to study nutrition. Regardless, we spent three days in Burlington, touring the school and exploring the area. Halfway through the trip, we went to a restaurant for dinner on Church Street. The waitress came to take our orders. My dad ordered one of those all-American burgers. My mom got fish tacos, and I ordered a salad. But not one of those grain salads, mozzarella-and-tomato stacked salads, or even one of those lettuce-filled bowls with a cup full of dressing. It was a simple garden salad that came with feta cheese, walnuts, and craisins, yet I asked for all those toppings to be taken off. Upon hearing my order, the waitress asked, "So, you basically want lettuce and chicken?"

To which I responded, "Yes, and dressing on the side please."

I did not have a true Church Street experience where people ate their way through the weekend farmer's market and enjoyed the creamy and delicious homemade ice cream from the Ben and Jerry's Tour. Instead, I declined all the foods my body truly craved.

September 2013

A few weeks later, on Labor Day weekend, I was scrolling through Pinterest, licking my lips at the endless possibilities of recipes I so desperately wanted to eat. I found one for an heirloom tomato pizza and decided to make it. Besides the fact that the crust was not going to fit into my diet regimen, I thought the healthiness of the tomatoes and sauce and lack of cheese made up for that. I prepared the recipe for dinner. I rolled out the ball of whole-grain dough, sprinkling the smallest amount of flour onto the granite countertop. I wrestled the dough into a perfect circle, not too thin that it would break through in the middle, but not too thick that it wouldn't feed all of us. Once the dough was rolled out just right, it crisped in the oven. I spread a thin layer of ricotta cheese onto the dough to act as glue and cut the heirloom tomatoes into perfect slices. I layered each slice—green, red, orange, yellow, and pink. It was a beautiful rainbow of tomatoes. The pizza cooked in the oven, and I cut it into eight slices. Next was angel food cake. I used a Betty Crocker mix and prepared the cake in a Bundt pan. It came out snow white, with a graham cracker-colored golden bottom.

When we all sat down for dinner, I took one slice of pizza. I brought the pizza up to my mouth. The heat steamed my face. The warmth made me excited to take a bite. I bit into the slice and the crunch of the crust sent flurries of crumbs onto my plate. It was the perfect combination of creaminess from the ricotta and sweetness from the tomatoes. I continued eating my slice of pizza, not wanting it to end. I was still finishing my first slice as my mom and dad were making their way onto their second and third. When I took my last bite, I wanted more than anything to have another slice, not wanting the deliciousness to end. But instead, I took my napkin, wiped the crumbs off my face, and pushed my plate away to reflect that I was done. And as I did this, my mom looked at me, rolled her eyes, and asked me if I was going to have another slice.

I said, "No."

After dinner, I went upstairs to my room. A few minutes later, there was a knock at my door. I was at my dresser, taking my earrings off and getting ready to put my pajamas on. My dad walked in as I stood against my dresser. He asked me if everything was all right. He didn't specify what "everything" was, and he didn't ask any follow-up questions. But it was very clear that "everything" was referring to my eating. I felt a wave of heat run through my body. My cheeks turned red, my heart started racing, and I felt tears welling in my eyes. I tried to wipe away the tears before they coated my cheeks, but they were coming out faster than my hands could move. I was able to choke out the words, "Everything is all right," as my mom walked in. My dad came in for a hug first. He wrapped his arms around my back. When he pulled away, my mom gave me a hug and a kiss on the forehead. But that was it. After the hug, we all went our separate ways. It was like a tree fell in the middle of the road, but instead of removing it, everyone just detoured around it for weeks and months on end until it turned into an even bigger problem.

I did have a piece of cake that night—one sixteenth of the cake because that was the serving size on the back of the Betty Crocker Angel Cake box—and you can bet I cut sixteen slices out of that cake before taking my slice.

Five months prior, I weighed 115 pounds and was thriving. Now, school was starting in a few days, and I was entering into my junior year of high school. None of my clothes fit. My size two American Eagle jean shorts fell down my legs. No belt could make them stay up on my hips. My spine protruded through my shirts. My thigh gap—something I worked extremely hard to get—was obvious. The hair on my arms was fuzzy and thin. The hair on my head fell out with a simple brush stroke. I was always cold, goosebumps adorning my arms, wrapped in a sweatshirt in prime New England heat. I never smiled. I was always on edge, ready to enter battle.

Entering my junior year, I weighed 96 pounds. And despite my significant weight loss and diminished mood, I felt on top of the world. The only problem was I hadn't gotten my period in four months. As someone who got their period every thirty-five days on the dot, I lost it almost immediately upon dieting. I thought it was kind of odd, but I never did anything about it. But once September rolled around, I told my mom. Was I unintentionally seeking help? Was I letting the cat out of the bag on purpose? Or was I really concerned about losing my period? I have no idea. But what I do know is that the moment I told my mom was the moment my world turned upside down. Junior year was not only the most important year of high school, but it was also supposed to be one of those bucket list years, with SATs and ACTs, college tours, and prom. It was supposed to be the year of late-night parties, dating, and maybe even some sneaking of alcohol. But this was all put on the back burner the moment I told my mom about my missed period.

Chapter Three

"Because here's what I believe: a child can survive a teacher or other children accidentally suggesting that he's not okay, as long as when he comes home, he looks at his mama and knows by her face that he really is okay. Because that's all they're asking, isn't it? Mama, am I okay?"

—GLENNON DOYLE

September 20, 2013

I sat on the doctor's bed in a paper hospital gown. My skinny, pale legs dangled off the edge and my frail, purple fingers fidgeted with the string on my gown. I gazed around the room. I had been in this room many times before. A Winnie the Pooh mural was painted on the four walls. Winnie the Pooh licked his honey-covered lips, while Piglet danced in the grass, Eeyore drunkenly teetered along, and Tigger hippity-hopped up and down. It brought back memories of my childhood and my stuffed animal "Piggy," with his half-ripped ears, faded color, and matted fur. As I continued looking around the room, I saw a canister above the sink. I squinted and as I moved my body forward the tissue paper-like covering on the exam table crinkled, a tear ripping beneath my hands. The more I moved forward to get a closer look at the canister, the more the paper shredded. Finally, and to my dismay, I realized the canister was filled with those extra-long Q-tips, the ones they use to test for strep throat. They were the Q-tips that make your throat feel a hundred times worse than when you originally walked into the doctor's office complaining of a sore throat.

It was a twofold memory. I hated getting a strep test as a child. I remember sitting on my mom's lap, bracing myself for an invasion of my throat. My body tense and rigid, eyes locking on the doctor's every move. The anticipation of the test was worse than the actual test. The doctor always made way for the outside of my throat first, poking and prodding their cold and alcohol-scented fingers around my throat, asking me to open and say, "Ahh." If the doctor could trick me fast enough, that quick opening of my month translated to a painful and unexpected swab of my tonsils, and then a fast pull out before my hands made their way to the Q-tip to ferociously pull it out. But, perhaps the best part or really the only good part about all of this was a positive test meant a trip to Wendy's for a chocolate frosty afterward because it created excitement on a somber day and what else felt better on a sore throat? I noticed myself licking my lips and before I even began to reimagine the coolness of the Frosty through my body, there was a knock at the door. My fingers started playing with the string faster, as my heartbeat became more rhythmic. Goosebumps made their way throughout my body.

Dr. O'Brien walked into the room. She had subtle gray hairs growing from her roots, as her dirty-blonde hair was perfectly parted down the middle. She wore a plaid, wool skirt. I was expecting Dr. O'Brien's typical welcome, which consisted of a smile as big as her face, eyes white and bulging, and a personality that arrived ten steps before she did. But she did not. This time, a frown adorned her face, and she presented as reserved. Before she even sat down or sanitized her hands, she shut the door and asked, "Sara, what is going on?"

My heart raced and my cheeks turned tomato red. I could feel the heat building in my face. A waterfall of tears streamed down my chin and onto the paper hospital gown, creating a damp texture. I rubbed my fingers on the water spots. Dr. O'Brien did not say anything. She let me cry and placed a box of Kleenex—the ones that feel like sandpaper—next to me. After going through half of the box, my face likely in need of lotion, Dr. O'Brien pulled the wheely chair from the desk and sat down in front of me. She put her hand on my knee and rubbed. For a moment, it seemed as though she peeled off her doctor's coat and put on her civilian's armor. Just as she paused the rubbing, our eyes interlocked. The motion of my quivering lips felt as though I was cascading up a wooden rollercoaster, knowing that at the top, something big was about to happen. But getting to the top was the hardest part. I had to build up the stamina to say what was going on. Just as I reached the top, my heart now pounding outside of my chest, I opened my mouth and screamed, as the cart descended. This time though, instead of screaming and grasping on for dear life, I buried my head in my hands and released a fresh stream of tears.

In between gasps of air, I croaked out, "I'm just so stressed out. I want to get all A's in my classes, but school is hard. Some of my teachers are strict." After I said my piece, I took my hands away and showed my face, as though I was a small child trying to hide to avoid punishment.

Dr. O'Brien looked at me and said, "That is understandable. Have you talked to your teachers?"

"Yes, I have been staying after school in math and Spanish to get extra help," I replied. "That is great! You are taking all of the right steps."

I nodded. There was a moment of silence. Dr. O'Brien looked at me. My eyes darted from each side of the room, trying to avoid making eye contact with her. The air in the room became tense. It felt as though we both knew what was going on. It was obvious I had lost weight and was now underweight. I came into this appointment because I lost my period and here I was trying to convince myself as well as my doctor that maybe my period magically disappeared because I was stressed out.

"Sara, do you think this stress is making it hard for you to eat?"

I shrugged my shoulders.

"Can I have your mom come in so the three of us can talk? I think it might be a good idea to talk to her about what is going on."

I nodded.

Dr. O'Brien stood up, pushed the wheely chair into the desk, and walked out of the room. A few minutes later, my mom and Dr. O'Brien arrived. My mom sat down on the stool in the corner of the room and Dr. O'Brien re-positioned herself in the chair. My mom's eyes traveled back and forth from Dr. O'Brien's to mine.

"Sara has lost quite a bit of weight over the last several months. I am concerned she is not eating enough."

My mom's face turned white. Her mouth opened, but no words came out. She got up from the stool and approached me, putting her hand on my shoulder to rub empathetically.

"I am going to give you a list of resources with nutritionists and therapists to look into. We can get through this."

There was a moment of silence. I do not know if Dr. O'Brien had another patient to see, if she just could not tolerate the silence, or if she knew she had to say something to break the density in the room. Whatever it was, she simply handed my mom a piece of paper filled with scribbles, stood up, and left. She did not even specify that I had developed an eating disorder. All she said was I lost a lot of weight.

I said nothing. I sat there, drained. There was not anything to say. The damage had been done and would only progressively get worse. I'm not sure why I said I lost weight because of stress and school. I think I was trying to say that my weight loss was a byproduct of stress and increased academic demand. At that point in time, I really did not know why I stopped eating. I wouldn't fully understand why I stopped eating until the end of my journey.

When my mom and I left the office, it was dark outside. There was a bitter chill in the air that made me wish I had a coat. We got in the car, and my mom leaned over the seat and hugged me. She said, "Sara, everything is going to be okay." From what I can remember, there was not a lot of discourse on the car ride home. It was my parent's wedding anniversary that day, and they had dinner reservations at an Italian bistro. When we walked into the house, my dad was in the kitchen. It seemed my dad was aware of what happened at the appointment because the mood was somber. My family did what we do best, and that was to continue not talking about what happened. Instead, my mom went upstairs and powdered her face while my dad laced his shoes. We got into the car and drove to the restaurant as if everything was normal and we were one big happy family.

Early October 2013

In the following weeks, my mom, like she always does, made lists upon lists of nutritionists and therapists in the area. She scanned the Blue Cross Blue Shield provider list like it was her only job. Lists were color coded, lists were organized, and lists were turned into even more lists. As for me, I remember saying that if and when I went to see a nutritionist, I would listen to them and I would follow what they said. I still wanted to pursue a nutrition degree in college, so I valued nutritionists. It also seemed like a magical quick fix. My mom found a nutrition practice a few towns over.

The following week we walked into the office. There was a small waiting area with a few chairs. Tara walked out to greet us. She didn't look like a dietician to me. She was tall with long, straight dark brown hair. She had short bangs, wide, bulging eyes, and a smile that wasn't easy to believe. She wore brown slacks that looked old and worn and a blue top that was way too small and had a stain on the stomach. She walked us back into her office, and we sat down. Behind my mom and I was a bookshelf, filled with empty food and snack boxes. The empty boxes represented all walks of the supermarket, including Cheez-Its, marinara sauce jars, Barilla Rigatoni, and Campbell's Chicken Noodle Soup.

I sat back and listened, while my mom and Tara did the talking.

Tara: "It's nice to meet you both. I recently opened this practice after leaving as a dietician dietician at the Inpatient Eating Disorder Program.. I have two young sons. I am looking forward to getting to know more about you, Sara."

Mom: "We are grateful to have an appointment. I called around to so many different places. We recently went to Sara's pediatrician after Sara lost her period over the summer. Her doctor was very concerned about her recent and rapid weight loss."

Tara: "Ah, I see. Sara, can you tell me a little more about why you lost weight over the summer? What have you been eating?"

Me: (Slumped back in the chair.) "I joined a gym and started tracking my food on My Fitness Pal. Then I lost my period."

Tara: "Do you know how much weight you have lost?"

Me: "Like around fifteen pounds."

Mom: "We were recently at the pediatrician, and she

weighed 96 pounds, down from 115 pounds at her physical back in November of last year."

Tara: "Okay. Sara, can you walk me through what a typical day of eating looks like for you?"

Me: "I eat cereal for breakfast, a sandwich for lunch, and then whatever is for dinner."

Mom: "Well, for dinner you have been eating yogurt. You have not been eating my meals."

Me: (Rolling my eyes.) "Sometimes I do."

Tara: "Can we try adding in some different foods over the next few weeks?"

Me: "Yeah, that's fine."

Tara: "What types of foods would you be comfortable adding in?"

Me: (Shrugging my shoulders.) "I don't know. I mean I haven't had chicken or potatoes in a while, and I really like both of those foods."

Tara: "Okay, great. How often do you think you can eat those foods during the week? Do you like pasta?"

Me: "I don't know, maybe chicken a few times a week and potatoes twice a week. I like pasta too, but I haven't had it in a long time."

Tara: "Can we try pasta once a week?"

Me: "Sure."

I agreed to eat:

Pasta - once a week

Potato - twice a week

Chicken - a few times per week

Tara also took my weight. The last time I personally took my weight was in September when the scale read 96 pounds. I would not know my weight for the next three-and-a-half years. From that point on, I was either told to step on the scale backward, or I requested not to be told.

Chapter Four

"So, feel what you need to feel. Release what you need to release, but keep the wisdom of the experience. Let it grow you. Let it show you what needs more work. Release the anger, but keep the lesson."

—EMILY MAROUTIAN

Mid-October 2013

Despite my agreement with Tara, I refused to eat anything other than what I had been eating for the last several months. I felt empowered by this newfound ability to ignore my hunger cues. The pain in my chest every morning thrilled me. It was a reminder that I was not only starving myself, but I was continuing to manipulate my own body. Instead of my body controlling me, I controlled it. I dictated when I was going to eat, not my hunger cues. I allowed myself to eat, not my body. It became a thrilling experience. An addiction.

A week later, I had my next appointment with Tara. As I sat in the waiting room, I stared at the rug beneath my feet. A feeling of doom set in. I felt as though I was in a principal's office after having done something wrong. The only "bad" thing I did that week was not eat what we agreed upon. But was that necessarily "bad"? My eating disorder voice said I had done exactly what I should have. As I sat there, silently, I could not help but wonder what this appointment would entail. But before I could even contemplate, I heard the shuffling of Tara's feet. She poked her head around the corner and said hello.

Tara: "Good morning. How are you both? If it is okay, I'd like to meet with Sara individually and then have you join us, Stacey."

Mom: "Yes, of course."

I shrugged and followed her. We walked into the office and just as I was about to sit down, Tara said, "Let's have you step on the scale. Backwards. You can take off your boots." *Oh boy, here we go.* Stepping on the scale backward only fueled my disorder. It angered me that neither Tara nor the doctors would let me see the number on the scale. It was my body. I deserved the right to know. If they were not going to let me know how much I weighed, then I sure as hell was not going to do what they said. I wanted to get back at Tara. I wanted to protect my disorder.

Tara: "How has this past week been?"

Me: "It's been okay."

Tara: (Big sigh.) "Okay, you can get off and put your shoes on. Take a seat. Were you able to eat any of the foods we talked about?"

Me: "Um… I had a piece of chicken the other night, but that was it."

Tara: "What about the pasta and potatoes?"

Me: "I didn't have it."

Tara: "How come?"

Me: (Shrugging my shoulders.) "I don't know."

Tara: "You look even thinner than you did last time I saw you, which was only a week ago. I mean look at you. You are wearing a long sleeve shirt, jeans, and a scarf and it's sixty-five degrees outside. You are not eating enough."

Me: (Silence. I stared back at her, tears beginning to fill my eyes. Why would she say something like that? Who cares what I was wearing? I liked my outfit. At least the clothes fit to a degree.)

Tara: "Well, I think it is a good idea to have your mom come in."

Me: "Okay."

Tara walked out of the room. I glanced at the clock, feeling as though the time was slowly ticking by. My mom walked into the room and looked at me, caressing her hand on my back. I assumed Tara told her I lost weight. Although Tara did not tell me I lost weight, her sigh, as I stepped off the scale, was big enough to insinuate this. My mom looked defeated. I think she felt like she failed that week as a parent. In her mind, me not gaining weight or even maintaining my weight was a reflection of her inability to intervene and parent me out of this eating disorder.

Tara: "Sara is not eating enough, so we need to create a plan to help her gain weight."

Mom: "Yes, okay."

Me: (Silence.)

Tara: "My first thought is to have Sara drink Ensure. They come in a few different flavors. I think chocolate, strawberry, and vanilla. It might be easier for you to consume, Sara, because it is a drink. My other thought is this sample of a food plan I have created for another client. They enjoy Mediterranean foods, so many of the foods and meal choices you see reflect that. This is something I will create for you today and email it to you every Sunday morning so that you have it for the week. If there are certain meals and foods you like, I can add them."

Mom: "This sounds good."

Tara: "What do you think, Sara?"

Me: "Okay."

Tara implemented a measurement and conversion meal plan. The plan categorized foods (i.e., starch, milk, vegetable, fruit, meat/protein, and fat) and allocated a certain number of portions per category. When Tara presented the example of the meal plan, it seemed okay initially. In one respect, it felt reassuring to know that the planning piece of things would be taken care of. But the next day, when Tara emailed my mom and I, it instantly became overwhelming. It set the precedent that Sunday mornings would be dedicated to math problems and equations that were impossible to solve.

Meal Plan for Sara - Week 1

Food Group	Servings per Day	Serving Sizes of Common Foods			
Starch • 1oz • 1 slice • ½ cup	4	1 slice bread or small roll	½ small bagel, English muffin	⅓ cup pasta, rice, or quinoa	¾–1 cup unsweetened cereal; 1oz granola *(plus ½ fat)*
		Flat-Out* bread *(1½ starch)*	1 small hamburger bun/hot dog roll	½ cup potatoes, corn, peas	2 4" pancakes; 1 4" waffle
		2 Deli Flats* halves ("1 roll")	½ 6" pita pocket; ½ 12" pita	1 small potato	3 cups popcorn; 4–6 crackers
Milk • 8oz	2	8oz Milk	6oz plain low-fat yogurt	6oz Yoplait OR Chobani Greek yogurt *(½ milk, 1 starch)*	

Vegetable • ½ cup cooked • 1 cup raw	2	½ cup cooked	1 cup raw	1 cup salad	½ cup juice
Fruit • ½ cup juice • 1 cup	2	1 medium piece of fruit	½ cup canned or sliced fruit	1 cup fresh fruit (large pieces), whole berries	¼ cup dried
Meat/ Protein • 1oz meat • ½ cup beans	5	1oz fish, poultry, beef, pork	1 whole egg, 2 egg whites	1oz cheese; 1 original Babybel cheese *(plus ½ fat)*	½ cup cooked beans/lentils *(plus 1 starch)*
		1 thin slice deli meat	1oz tofu	¼ cup cottage cheese	2 TBSP peanut butter *(plus 1 fat)*
Fat • 1 tsp	4	1 tsp oil, margarine, butter, mayo	1 TBSP salad dressing (regular)	⅛ or 1oz avocado	8-10 olives
		1 TBSP cream cheese, sour cream, cream	2 TBSP light salad dressing	1 strip bacon	6-10 nuts; 1 TBSP seeds

Serving Size Guidelines

1 cup = baseball	1 oz / 2 tbsp / ⅛ cup = golf ball	3 oz meat = deck of cards
¾ cup = tennis ball	1 TBSP / 3 tsp = poker chip	3 oz fish = checkbook
½ cup = light bulb	1 tsp = quarter	1 oz deli meat = CD

46

Sample Daily Plan

Breakfast	1 Starch 1 Milk 1 Fruit	1 cup Special K cereal 8 oz milk ½ cup sliced strawberries
Snack	1 Starch 1 Milk	Ensure Nutrition Shake -
Lunch	1 Starch 2 Protein 1½ Fats	Deli Flats* ("1 roll" or 2 halves) 2 slices deli meat 1 Original Babybel cheese ⅛ avocado
Snack	1 Fruit 1 ½ Fat	1 apple 9 almonds
Dinner	1 Starch 2 Vegetables 3 Protein 1 Fat	½ cup mashed sweet potatoes 1 cup cooked vegetables 3oz chicken breast 1 teaspoon olive oil

Sample Daily Plan

Breakfast	1 Starch ½ Milk 1 Fruit	¾ cup Bran cereal 4 oz milk 2 tablespoons raisins
Lunch	1 Starch 2 Protein 1 Fat	Deli Flats* ("1 roll" or 2 halves) 2-3 slices deli meat 1 teaspoon mayo
Snack	1 Starch ½ Milk 1½ Fat	Greek yogurt - 6 walnut halves
Dinner	1 Starch 2 Vegetables Protein 1½ Fat 1 Milk 1 "Fruit"	½ cup soba noodles (for stir-fry) 1 cup cooked vegetables 3oz chicken 1½ teaspoons peanut oil 8 oz milk 1 Tablespoon chocolate syrup

Sample Daily Plan

Breakfast	3 Starch 1 Milk	Nature Valley "Crunch" granola bar or Fiber One bar 8 oz Ensure Nutrition Shake
Lunch	1 Milk 1 Fruit 1 Protein 1 Fat	6oz plain, yogurt ½ banana, sliced 2 tablespoons peanut butter -
Snack	1 Fruit 1 Fat	2 tablespoons raisins 6 almonds
Dinner	1 Starch 2 Vegetables 4 Protein 2 Fat	⅓ cup brown rice 1 cup cooked vegetables 4oz fish 2 teaspoons margarine

So, on Sunday mornings I sat in the corner of our living room couch, curled up in a blanket, while my mom sat next to me, pen and paper in hand. As the *Today Show* played in the background, my mom and I spent hours planning every meal I would eat for the week, including breakfast, lunch, dinner, and one snack. From eight until ten-thirty a.m., sometimes longer, we planned everything. I was planning snacks I would be eating three days in advance, forcing myself to try foods that I did not and had never liked, and becoming more and more afraid of the very thing I truly needed—food. I was measuring everything I ate, from one tablespoon of oil to an eighth of an avocado, to half of a large banana. The kitchen countertops were covered with measuring spoons and cups and food scales. Although I was measuring some foods over the summer, I had not engaged in such restrictive rituals leading up to working with Tara. Grocery store trips were equally overwhelming. As we walked up and down the aisles, my eyes gazed at the various foods I so desperately craved. I felt like a kid in a candy store, pointing to everything, wanting it all, but knowing I could not actually have it all. Or perhaps, I could have it all, I just wouldn't allow myself to.

At times, there were grocery trips in which I really wanted to try different foods. When I wanted to try something new, my mom emailed Tara because *obviously* we needed to know where the food fit in on the meal plan.

Email on 10/28/13:

Hi Tara,

These are the things she likes/wants to be able to eat (some of which you've already taken care of). She is definitely looking for more variety now.

- *Chobani with granola for lunch*
- *Whole milk*
- *Ensure as a snack*
- *Ensure with granola bar (1 bar) for breakfast*
- *Waffles*
- *Cereal*

- *Wrap sandwich, hummus and veggies*
- *Pretzels*
- *Pasta*
- *Beef*

Her "dream dinners" are salmon with pesto, pasta & veggies, and tacos!

She really enjoyed her sandwich on Sunday with 2 slices of whole wheat bread, however, having 4 starches between breakfast, snack, and lunch, made it impossible for her to have a starch at dinner. She ate everything else and told me later that she would have been comfortable having even more protein at dinnertime. (The protein was shrimp.)

Stacey

Sometimes Tara emailed back in a timely manner and other times we never got a response, which meant I was not trying anything new that week. If anything, the plan instantly made me feel more food constrained. Now that foods had a label and there was a limit on the amount of foods I could eat, it fueled my eating disorder. Tara's plan reiterated to me that I needed to be on some form of a diet and that food must be restricted. Tara's model of recovery was a clear indicator that I was not going to get better. I was only going to get worse.

Late October 2013

In the midst of all of this, I was a junior in high school. Maintaining friendships was challenging, and I could not tolerate the uncertainty of what being around friends entailed. Hanging out with friends equated to junk food, food that only provoked my anxiety. There was a part of me that wanted to be honest and let my friends in. At times, it felt more painful to refrain from telling them about my eating disorder than it would have been to just tell them. I did not have faith they would understand. We were at a stage in our lives where we were all so obsessed with ourselves. Our age-normative ignorance tarnished our capacity to empathize. Not to mention, we all constructed our own definitions of "healthy" and danced around patterns of disordered eating. We were sixteen years old. In a way, it was deemed normal to have negative thoughts about food. Regardless, my friendships became inconsistent. I saved myself for one or two nights a month to be with them. That was all my mind and body could handle.

One Saturday afternoon, three of my friends invited me to the mall. Although shopping, once a weekly outing, was no longer pleasurable, I decided to go. It was a way to maintain a sense of normalcy. As Kristen drove, music blaring, I could feel myself succumbing to a sensory overload. It was so loud I could not even hear my eating disorder. I stared out the window, each pothole in the road waking me up from my daze. When we arrived at the mall, I had all of two seconds to reclaim myself before we walked in, lights shining bright. The lighting was intense and blinding. It was as though we were walking onto a runway. I squinted so my body could adjust, a clear indicator that I had not been to a store in a long time. And if the lights were not enough, the smell was just as overpowering. I was instantly hit with the smell of soft-baked pretzels from Auntie Annie's. People walked by with pretzels as big as their faces. I could feel my tongue start to move, as though it was getting ready to lick the salt.

As we walked through the mall, I looked side-to-side, taking everything in. I almost forgot what the experience was like. Kiosks in the center with people trying to make an awkward sales pitch: "Try our amazing new flat iron. Your hair will never look so straight!"

"Over here, Miss! Let me give you a massage."

"Looking for an excursion to the Caribbean? Take a look at one of our brochures!"

And if the act of merely walking through the mall was not overwhelming enough, I did not prepare myself for department store employees to accost me with the plethora of perfume samples. It was like an obstacle course, trying to dodge through everyone.

Finally, we reached our favorite stores. Bath and Body Works was a must. We smelled our way around the store, stocking up on soap and hand sanitizer. "Hey guys, do you want to get something to eat after?" Elizabeth asked. "Yeah, sure!" Emma exclaimed. "Yes, I want to get some food, too," said Kristen. I continued looking around the store, hoping my silence was loud enough. Kristen turned to me and asked, "What are you going to get for lunch?" Still looking at the body lotions, I said, "I ate before so I'm not hungry right now." "Well you have some time to think about it," said Kristen. I shrugged my shoulders.

After we checked out, we walked over to the food court. All we had to do was follow the smell to find the food court. Cooks walked around with trays of teriyaki chicken, while people stood in line with platefuls of lo mein and fried rice. French fries seemed to cover the floor underneath the tables, likely dropped by children, too busy enough to notice they were missing their mouths. I felt as though my body was covered in grease just by standing at the center of the food court.

"What are you guys going to get?" asked Kristen. "I'm going to get a hamburger and French fries," Elizabeth replied. "I'm going to get a slice of pizza, I think," said Emma. As we walked through the food court, Kristen asked me, again, "Sara, what are you going to get?" "I ate before we came. I'm not hungry." "All right, well if you change your mind, that's okay. You can always get something and then just not eat tomorrow," Kristen offered.

You can just get something and then not eat tomorrow.
You can just get something and then not eat tomorrow.
You can just get something and then not eat tomorrow.

Had I heard her correctly? Did she really just say I can get something and then not eat the next day? Was she serious? It was one thing for me to give myself that advice, but it was completely different for someone else. And Kristen knew what I was going through. I opened up to her a few weeks before. It was a brief conversation as we walked through the hallway at school. I blurted it out randomly and unintentionally. I had not meant to tell her. It just sort of happened, and once it was out there, I could not take it back. To my surprise, Kristen empathized with me when I told her. She related to what I was going through, which made her comment at the mall that much more concerning. Was I triggering her? What provoked her to say that? Did she think that comment would make me feel better?

My emotions were like a colorful rubber band ball—red represented my frustration and anger, blue was my sadness, yellow the guilt for going to the mall in the first place, and purple for my desire to feel relief from my disorder. No one understood my eating disorder but me and my disorder. I shut down after Kristen said that. I wanted to go home.

"Hey, guys, do you mind if we get going? I'm not feeling too great," I said. "Yes. Are you okay?" asked Elizabeth. "I just have a headache and want to lay down," I said.

My experience at the mall that day was proof that surrounding myself with friends was more agonizing than being alone. Being with people meant resisting food cravings, fabricating lies as to why I couldn't eat, and fighting against the anxiety of not wanting to be out with friends in the first place. Continuing to fall deeper into my eating disorder proved easier.

I succumbed to constant hibernation, retreating deeper within myself. And as I pulled away from my friends, they did not seem to miss me. If anything, the invitations to hang out seemed to dissipate almost completely. I had consistently showed up for my friends in the past. Why wouldn't they do the same? If they did not need me, then did the world even need me?

November 2013

As I strangely embraced my freedom from friends, days turned into weeks. Sunday evenings began the countdown for a dreadful five days to come. Wednesdays emphasized the halfway point, shedding a glimmer of hope. And although Friday brought a light at the end of the tunnel, the gloom of Friday evenings and Saturday mornings seemed to blur this.

Every Friday after school I met with Dr. O'Brien. The appointments were monotonous. First, the nurse called my name from the waiting room. I would give my mom the same tearful look. The nurse would grab my shoulder, guide me backward onto the scale, and instruct me to take my shoes off. Fighting with the bar on the scale to get it even, it felt as though the nurse was inadvertently taking out her frustration with the task on me. Eventually, she would ask me to step off the scale and go into the room. Then, after fumbling around with the blood pressure pump, she would say, "Ugh, let me get a smaller one." After trying on endless pumps, she would finally find one that fit. She would then instruct me to lay down for five minutes and then she would take my pulse. After that, I had to sit up for five minutes and have my pulse taken again. Then I would stand up for another five minutes and have my pulse taken one last time.

Unsurprisingly, each position led to a significant decrease in my heartrate and an increased light-headedness. The nurse always ended her symphony of orders with: "Strip your clothes off and put on the gown. Dr. O'Brien will be in soon."

Despite my own role in my eating disorder and the sick part of me that wanted to continue losing weight, the real Sara, the true and healthy Sara, was still in there. And she wanted to, no, she *deserved* to be treated with respect. If anything, she did not need another person judging her for this disorder. She needed someone to empathize and to tell her, "Darling, it's going to be okay." If I walked into that doctor's office as a five-year-old with a runny nose, I would be told, "Sweetie, you are going to feel better soon. Mom, give her some Tylenol and make sure she gets rest." I still needed that. I needed that medicine of love and kindness, not just from my mom but from medical professionals as well.

After taking off my clothes, I would sit on the bed and to both my dismay and relief I would hear a knock on the door. "Hello, Sara. How are you feeling?" Before I could answer, Dr. O'Brien would blurt a myriad of questions, including, "What are you eating? How are your appointments with Tara? Do you think you could try and eat a bite of a peanut butter and jelly sandwich? It could be one tiny bite? Just a small piece? I want to try and get you to eat more."

My response was always the same: a blank stare. Either Dr. O'Brien was completely robbed of social skills, or she did not care to take a breath in between questions because despite my lack of engagement, she kept going. Reaching Friday was a victory in and of itself. I was in no capacity to listen, talk, or take in any more information, let alone discuss the very thing that was defeating me every day. If eating was hard, talking about eating was even harder. I needed rest. My mind needed rest. Dr. O'Brien would then invite my mom into the room and repeat the same information she shared with me—Sara needs to eat more. And that was it. She would send us on our way, just like she always did.

As for Saturday mornings, they continued to be reserved for appointments with Tara.

By November, I had already succumbed to Ensure, a thick and chalky drink of pure muck. It smelled of chemicals and the long list of ingredients on the back looked far from what one would consider nutritious. Ensure was both a punishment and lifeline. On the one hand, if I was not going to eat my calories, I had to drink them, which felt both wrong and torturous. But on the other hand, the less I was eating, the more I was dying, and Ensure was a quick fix to help me survive. The hardest part about drinking Ensure was that deep down I wanted to learn to befriend food again, and drinking Ensure only prevented me from doing that. It was as though Tara had no faith in me and it was easier to give me a high calorie drink rather than take the time to truly help me recover.

If Ensure seemed to contradict my recovery, then Tara's way of adding cake to my repertoire was of the utmost contradiction. Cake was a celebratory food for my seventeenth birthday, and

I wanted nothing more than to indulge in its deliciousness. Although Tara incorporated the cake into my plan, she provided a specific measurement of the size of cake I could eat. One two-inch slice of square cake, to be exact. If Tara really wanted to help me recover and normalize my feelings around food, then she sure as hell would not have given me a specific size of cake I could eat. And because my disorder held me captive to the meal plan and measurements, I used a tape measure to cut a two-inch slice of cake.

Birthday Plan

Breakfast	1 Starch 1 Milk 1 Fruit	1 cup Special K cereal 8 oz whole milk ½ cup sliced strawberries
Snack	2 Fruit	1 large banana
Lunch	1 Starch 2 Protein 1 Vegetable 1 Fat 1 Milk	Deli Flat 2-3 slices deli meat 1 cup sliced Bell peppers 1 tsp mayo 8 oz whole milk
Dinner	1 Starch 1 Vegetable 3 Protein 1 Milk 1 Fat	⅓ cup quinoa ½ cup cooked vegetable 3 oz salmon 8 oz whole milk 1 tsp oil
Dessert	2 Starch 1 Fat	2" square of cake with frosting -

My work with Tara made me sicker. She gave my eating disorder the ammunition it needed to continue taking over my mind and body. Measurements, sizes, and numbers consumed my mind. In three short months, I became more hyper focused around food and calories than I had been my entire life.

Mid-November 2013

Despite my health crisis, I was still a junior in high school, and I had plans of going to college and being someone someday. I still had my mind set on nutrition, despite my current mental and physical state. At my next appointment with Tara, we talked about the upcoming trip because for some reason, we continued to seek approval from Tara to engage in normal activities.

Mom: "We have a trip planned to visit UMAINE and take a college tour next weekend. Our plan is to pack food for Sara so that she can stay on track with the meal plan."

Tara: "Hmm. I would really think about this trip and consider your options. I'm not sure now is the best time."

Me: (Silence.)

Mom: "I understand what you are saying, but I think my husband and I really want Sara to have some of these normal experiences despite what she is going through."

Tara: "Okay. There is time to think about it. You can let me know. We can hold off on meeting next week, and you can let me know."

Mom: "Okay."

Me: (Silence.)

Nevertheless, we went on the trip that following Friday. It was a five-hour drive to Bangor, Maine, and we packed three days' worth of food for me. We brought food scales, measuring cups, spoons, bowls, and plates. The trunk of the car was a portable supermarket. As I bundled up in the backseat, I could not help but wonder what my life would be like when I went to college. Would I still have an eating disorder? Would I just continue following Tara's guidelines and charts? Would I have a boyfriend? Would I have friends? As my mind began to formulate answers, I felt myself doze off. Sometimes just thinking about the future exhausted me. I was so depleted of energy I could barely get through the day. Sleep allowed me to rest, both physically and mentally. But a bump on the highway quickly awakened me, and I realized my dad was turning into a parking lot.

"Sara, we are going to stop for a bit to get some dinner. Dad is going to go inside to Panera and get us something to eat. Are you sure you don't want anything?" said my mom. "No, I'm okay," I said.

My mom opened the trunk and pulled out a container of salad. It was a garden salad with lettuce, cucumbers, and carrots. I ate my dinner, one forkful at a time, crunching away on lettuce, slowly eating each bite. Eating was ritualistic. It was important I ate slow so that I could savor the food for I knew it would be a while before I could eat again. As I ate, I could see the steam from the roll my mom was eating warm her face. It was a white baguette, buttery on the inside and crispy on the outside. The crumbs from the bread dressed her salad. My dad slurped away on his chicken noodle soup, dipping the bread in the broth, creating a delectable sogginess. Just a year ago, I, too, would have been eating those exact same things. But here I was, measuring a quarter cup of cucumbers for my salad.

We arrived at the hotel late that night and awoke early the following morning. Before leaving for the campus tour, my mom and I prepared my lunch for the day. I did not let my mom make my meals without my help. I feared she would make me fat. Maybe she would purposely put on too much avocado or add in an extra tablespoon of oil. Even worse, she might try and use white bread instead of wheat. As I hovered over her in the hotel room, I watched as she made the turkey and avocado wrap. "That's too much avocado! Take some off!" I said. "Sara, that is exactly an ⅛, which is what Tara put on the plan." I fought back tears as they filled my eyes. "That's too much," I cried, as I began to reach for the knife. My mom, seemingly frustrated, evidenced by her eye roll and quick tone snapped, "Sara, if you take any more off, there won't be any avocado on the wrap. "No! I'm taking some off," I said. I wiped off almost all the avocado, which was not a lot to begin with. All that was left was a small smear, barely visible. My mom sighed. "Do you want to put the turkey on, then?" "Yes," I said, reaching for the turkey. As I strategically placed the turkey breast, my mom interrupted. "Sara, that's not enough. You barely have any turkey left on the sandwich." "No, it's fine!" I said. My mom sighed.

By the end of the campus tour and the trip itself, my legs were out of order, my cheeks hurt from the bitter air, and my body was depleted. The trip reiterated that I was not getting better, and, in fact, I was becoming sicker. As I grew sicker, Tara's guidelines seemed to become more rigid, and there was less room for creativity.

Email on 11/18/13:

Panko breadcrumbs are 1 oz. or ½ cup 1 starch?

She [Sara] saw a berry cream cheese in the super-market… does this count as 1 fat?

BBQ sauce—where does this fit in? She [Sara] would probably have a tablespoon.

Stacey

Response to email on 11/18/23:

> *For the berry cream cheese, I will let Sara choose one or the other (but she needs to stick with one and not switch off): Either 1 TBSP = 1 fat (2 TBSP = 2 fat) OR 2 TBSP = 1 fat, ½ starch*
>
> *1 TBSP BBQ sauce = 1 fruit*
>
> *Panko = either 1/2 cup or 1oz (this is the same amount by weight and volume)*
>
> *Tara*

Having to decide on a Sunday if I wanted berry cream cheese to be 1 fat or 1 fat and a ½ starch for a meal on Wednesday was too much. It was easier to skip the berry cream cheese all together and stick with foods that fell into only one food category. I felt as though I was being forced to eat foods that I did not and had never truly enjoyed. I was never a peanut butter connoisseur, an avocado maniac, or even a frequent flyer in the dairy aisle. But now I was being forced to eat foods because of their caloric density. If anything, it made me want to ditch food all together. It was all becoming too overwhelming, too stressful, and too draining. The purpose of me going to see Tara was to gain weight and confidence around food and the exact opposite was happening.

Email on 12/16/13

Hi Tara,

Sara didn't have a good week at all. She saw the pediatrician on 12/12 and weighed 86 lbs. That night we were sent to Norwood Hospital for blood work and an EKG. Dr. O'Brien wanted to start her on Celexa but was concerned about her low heart rate (48). She got the okay to begin the medication and started it on Saturday.

Sara is bored with the food she's been eating for the past 6 months, but has spent so much time convincing herself that so many foods are "bad", that she's having a very difficult time introducing foods back into her life.

She's told me that she's tired of the whole situation and wants it to be "fixed". She's tired of feeling cold, tired, and hungry. She's scared and upset that her hair is falling out.

Thank you,
Stacey

Email on 12/17/13

Ok. She will start to feel better (physically and emotionally) once she is at a better state nutritionally. The problem is that she has been very resistant to move forward in her meal plans (I know she wants to though).

I think her eating disorder is using "boredom" as an excuse. Just tell her she needs to get through this and she will start to feel better. Her hair is falling out because she is not eating enough. She is cold, tired, and hungry because she is not eating enough. Please reiterate this to her (I know she knows it, but she may just need to hear it).

The most important thing right now is to get her to a stable place—weight loss, emergency blood work, and EKGs are not a stable place. She must eat everything (starches and fats included) on the meal plan in the upcoming week. This is very important—she is not going to get better unless she eats what I have prescribed. If she can't do it, then we may need to discuss with Dr. O'Brien getting Sara help with a higher level of support.

Tara

If she can't do it, then we may need to discuss with Dr. O'Brien getting Sara help with a higher level of support.

If she can't do it, then we may need to discuss with Dr. O'Brien getting Sara help with a higher level of support.

If she can't do it, then we may need to discuss with Dr. O'Brien getting Sara help with a higher level of support.

My mom had not shared that email exchange with me until years later, but I did not need to read it to know something felt different at my next appointment with Tara. As we sat in the waiting room, I stared off, a feeling of resentment blurring my ability to remain present. When Tara walked into the waiting room, she looked exhausted. From the bags under her eyes to her hunched over stance, she looked defeated. As I stood up, ready to follow her into her office, she said, "Stacey, why don't you come in as well."

Looking surprised herself, my mom replied, "Oh, okay." I felt like I was in the principal's office, waiting to be reprimanded for having done something wrong. The discomfort in the room was palpable. Each moment of silence was interrupted by the distant ticking of the clock. Tara appeared to shuffle papers around on her desk to manage the awkward silence while I tapped my fingers, one by one, against my thumb. The stiffness in the room was abruptly interrupted as Tara began her decent into intimidation.

Tara: "Sara, you have not been able to follow the meal plan, and you cannot continue on this path. We might need to consider other options."

Mom: "I'm…"

Tara: (Interrupting.) "There are many inpatient programs."

Me: (Sobbing.) "No. No. No. You can't do this. I'm not going anywhere."

Mom: (Fighting back tears and holding my hand.) "Where is this…"

Tara: (Interrupting.) "Sara needs to gain weight. An inpatient program might be our best option to help her achieve this goal. It is clearly too challenging for Sara to do this at home. She needs an increased level of care."

Me: (Sobbing.) "No. No. No."

Mom: (Silence.)

Me: (Sobbing.) "I promise I will eat, Mom. Don't send me. No. Please no."

Tara: (Staring at us blankly.)

Mom: (Wiping her eyes.) "I need to think this through."

Me: "No. Please no. Please no. Don't do this."

Tara: "I think that is a good idea, Stacey. I can have a conversation with Dr. O'Brien as well."

Was Tara giving up on me? Was I too weak to fight this? If Tara could not help me, then who could? Was I even worth fighting for? I wondered. Tara threatened me. She tried to scare me out of my eating disorder. The problem was I could not be saved. My thoughts were *eating* my mind. My disorder was *eating* my body. And my body was physically *eating* itself. Food was failing to be my medicine, and threats were not the nourishment I needed. The hospital was surely out of the question. My mind was like a game of fifty-two pickup. The cards facing up were the emotions I became. At times, I felt angry with my mom. I blamed her for this horrible disorder and for not doing anything to stop it. As I pushed away, my mom came in closer. She too felt anger and frustration. Our resentment toward the situation, however, often turned into enmeshment when we both needed consoling and reassurance that everything was going to be okay.

My mom feared the direction our relationship was going. She knew sending me to the hospital would only push me further away. She was not willing to risk that. Her fear, intertwined with my increased reassurance that I would eat more, ultimately led to us not driving to the hospital and admitting me into an inpatient program that day. At least, for the time being.

Everyone in my life at the time was trying to throw my body life rafts. Dr. O'Brien checked my pulse to ensure my heartbeat was healthy. Tara wanted me to eat more so my body would not wither away. My dad kept a passive distance, knowing he was not emotionally equipped to manage my sudden mood changes. And my mom took on the role of doctor, nurse, friend, and nutritionist, while still just trying to be a mom. But even that was not enough.

That Saturday morning, I thought I was smooth sailing, however, a wave brewed in the distance. It slowly rolled closer, getting bigger and accumulating more power, taking over, threatening to crash my boat into pieces. Tara slowly built up this wave, using her power to try and control my disorder. And when she could no longer fight against it, she decided to threaten me, crashing my boat in pieces. There were too many pieces to clean up. Frustration, anger, sadness, fear, anxiety, and resentment lay everywhere. Who would help me now? Could I even be helped?

Chapter Five

"My only choice was to fight my way out, even if I didn't think I would make it."

—Laurie Halse Anderson

January 2014

Just like my body, my world continued to shrink. I was confined to the thoughts of my mind. Every physical step further debilitated my body. Although Tara's existence was no longer present in my life, I still had weekly appointments with Dr. O'Brien. One evening in early January, Dr. O'Brien sent me to the emergency room. My heart rate was low. As my mom drove to the hospital, all I could think about was the test in school I had the next day. I spent weeks studying and preparing for the exam. It was a unit test and there was going to be a lot of material on it. I needed one last night to review everything. I did not care that my heart rate was low or that my body was signaling to me it needed to be cared for. I was only focused on the test.

As I sat on the hospital bed, distracted by the beeping sounds and monitors, my mom and dad sat staring at me, fear masking their faces. The doctor walked in with a domineering stance. He looked at my parents first and then glanced at me. I sat there with my legs as thin as twigs dangling off the bed. The doctor firmly pressed his stethoscope on my chest. I could feel every movement of the stethoscope on my body as it moved over my protruding bones. He stepped back, leaned against the counter, and said, "You do know people die from this? From eating disorders. You should eat more." I looked at him then at the clock and said, "Can I go home now?" My heart rate was not deemed low enough that I needed to be admitted, and given that the doctor had shared his medical "advice," there was not much left for the hospital to do. So, off I went.

Doctors did not know what to say. They did not know how to treat me or my disorder. They did not care to understand me. They never took the time to learn how I got sick. All they cared about was numbers. What rate was my heart beating at? What number did the scale reveal? How many calories was I eating? Did they not realize that numbers were what got me here in the first place? Calorie counting from the My Fitness Pal app perpetuated this disorder. Tara created some fucked-up meal plan that only added to my rigidity. And here we were again, basing my physical health off some stupid number. If anyone really wanted to take the time to treat me, they would have taken a moment to walk through the thoughts in my head. That was the real problem. My thoughts—my distorted perception of myself—was what got me here in the first place. It was not the physical exercise or the food I was eating, it was my mindset. It was my inability to see the beauty within myself.

Over the course of the next few months, I continued to regress, and things got worse. I became desensitized to hunger. If I stood up too fast, my legs became Jell-O and quickly gave out on me. At times, I collapsed to the floor, nearly hitting my head on furniture. Panic attacks became routine throughout the day, leading to my mouth foaming, my legs shaking, and my head throbbing from migraines. I could no longer drive when I could potentially pass out or have a panic attack. My mom drove me to and from school every day. I wore heating pads in my mittens and shoes. My body was in a constant state of cold. Goosebumps blanketed my body and the brief press of my fingers polished them in purple. A simple stroke of the hairbrush pulled out clumps of thin and ragged hair. I hid underneath leggings, sweatshirts, and blankets. My body was frail and thin. I had no figure. I was so afraid and so deprived of food that my body was physically deteriorating.

Family dinners were non-existent. My dad and I stopped talking, and I could no longer tolerate being in the same room as him. He became so frustrated, not with me, but with my disorder. My disorder impacted my ability to perceive things clearly. I was in a constant state of emotional dysregulation. Things that I once easily would have moved on from became more difficult to ignore. Disagreements erupted frequently and fights led to more fights. If I got upset that my mom potentially added too much oil in the pan, I instantly broke out in tears. It sent panic through my body. My dad could not handle it. He often retreated in his office in the basement. I planned when I would move about the house to not bump into him, and we barely made eye contact. Whether it was our own stubbornness or fear of what was happening, my dad and I did not speak. I think he felt helpless. I felt helpless. There was nothing he could do to save his little girl. The more he got frustrated, the more I pulled away. I was not equipped with the emotional capacity to handle my own frustration, let alone his.

And while my dad and I drifted apart, despite my mom and I's constant arguing, we somehow stuck together. Unlike the others, my mom kept on throwing me that life raft. Even when I fell apart, she was there. She was my blanket through my disorder. She slept with me every night, staring at the ceiling, praying, wishing, and hoping, somehow and someway, I would be free from this disorder.

Letter from my mom on 1/8/14:

Sara,

I want you to know how much I love you. I want you to know that you bring joy to me each and every day and have since the day you were born, and I held you in my arms. I want you to know that I am blessed and privileged to have you as my daughter. You have passion and strength. You are compassionate and caring. You are beautiful. You are smart. You are a gift and I treasure each and every moment with you.

I also want you to know that I am sorry for my mistakes. I'm sorry for not supporting you when you needed it most. I hate to see you suffering and depriving yourself. It pains me to see you sad.

You have been suffering for far too long and your body and soul are tired of this. It's 3 in the morning and I'd like to go into your room and wake you up to hold and comfort you. You sleep so peacefully tonight, so instead I decided to write down what I'd like to say.... I was [also] wrong for not telling you last summer that the exercising was too much or that you were eating too little. If I knew then what I know now I would change so many things. I can't change the past, but I can make things better and I can help you get better. I will never stop loving and caring about you. I will never give up. I will always be here—right here—for you.

You have been struggling for too many months and you deserve for this to be over. It needs to be over so that you can get your life back and enjoy each day. I will not allow anyone to hurt you—whether it's a teacher or friend or family member, or me. I will not hurt you. But I also don't want you to hurt yourself any longer. I don't want and will not allow this eating disorder to hurt you physically or emotionally. You have been through enough. The doctor's appointments and medical tests and panic attacks—you don't deserve this. You deserve so much more...

I know you want to get better, and I see each day how hard you work to reach that goal. I wish there were a magic spell I could cast to make this go away. I wish all the love I have for you could make it go away. I want you to know and believe in your heart that I love you. I want you to get better. It is time for you to put yourself first and get better, and I will be there every step of the way. You have an important and meaningful life to live and lots of love to give and it's time you put yourself first, to take care of yourself and get better. You deserve to be well.

I love you Sara and while my words may seem a bit random and scattered at this hour, they're words from my heart. Words I only have for you—the most special words for the most special person in my life—my daughter— you! I love you.

Love,

Mom

February 2014

As the bitterness of winter set in, I experienced minor epiphanies where bouts of wanting to recover crept in. At some point throughout my disorder, I had purchased *8 Keys to Recovery from an Eating Disorder* by Carolyn Costin and Gwen Schubert Grabb. After I bought the book, it merely collected dust. One day, however, during one of my random and rapid inclinations to get better, I picked it up. It felt impulsive. I was not sure what I was getting myself into. I think it was my curiosity. How "easy" was it to recover? And what did recovery entail? Did I just need to eat more? That was scary. After I read the first assignment in the book, I took out my journal, something that was also collecting dust, and wrote.

Journal entry on 2/8/14:

Hello Sara,

I don't know where to begin. Never have I ever imagined myself in the place I am today. Unhappy! Depressed! Stressed! Anxious! Mad at ones I thought I loved! Helpless! Hopeless! Alone! Sad! And most of all fighting and battling an eating disorder! The purpose of this journal is solely to help me and no one else. As of right now I am seeing a therapist and my doctor. Some visits are good and some not so good. But, like everyone tells me, I will take one step forward and two steps back. My goal of journaling is to help with my fighting and battling this eating disorder. So, today, February 8, 2014, at 10:26 a.m., I begin.

I just started reading 8 Keys to Recovery from an Eating Disorder and my first assignment is to write about the worst day I have had with this eating disorder. For me, I cannot solely pick one day, as each has brought their own challenges. But what I can say is that I am tired of measuring food! Tired of thinking about food! Tired of avoiding food! Tired of planning around food! And most of all, tired of being tired! I so want to find the "new and improved" Sara. The Sara without an eating disorder, or moreover, the Sara who can and will overcome this eating disorder! Today is the day. And although I know some days will be more strenuous than others, I know I have the strength to get through it.

Over the next month, I continued to read the book. At times, the act of journaling led to the perseveration of why and how I got stuck with an eating disorder in the first place. Although writing my thoughts seemed to help, it also frustrated me. Each thought reminded me of what I was going through and the trajectory my life was taking. On top of that, because of my linear personality, I felt like I *had* to finish reading a chapter of the book or complete an assignment merely because that was the expected thing to do. I was going through the physical task of reading, but I was not mentally retaining information. And, above all, writing was a lot easier than doing. My journal entries often contradicted my actions. It was easy to write about how I was going to eat more, what I was going to eat more of, and how I was going to learn to work through my emotions. But it was a lot harder to implement such tasks. Learning how to recover was hard.

March 2014

As I continued to move through the process of journaling and reading, I considered alternative therapies. I researched, "What can help someone recover from an eating disorder." Yoga was a common recovery model within the eating disorder community, and it seemed to populate my search. Something about the practice intrigued me. The photos of yoga studios looked inviting and warm. It seemed like a safe space with no mirrors. The yogis in the photos looked elegant and graceful in their poses. There was so much variety throughout the yoga community.

Fortunately, after a simple search, I found a local studio. I had never practiced yoga and although I was eager to learn the practice, I was not comfortable joining a class. After connecting with a teacher at the studio who facilitated private yoga sessions, my journey into the yoga world began.

The first time I stepped foot in the studio, I felt a warmth of physical and emotional energy. The studio was heated and a deep humidity permeated the air. The floor was cushioned, and windowed walls enclosed the studio space. A mat was set up at the front of the room, a bolster laying horizontal and two blocks at the end of the mat. Music played in the distance. But more than the warmth of the physical space was the warmth of the energy. My yoga instructor, Laura, created an ambiance of calmness. There was a sense of stillness in the room as she walked in. She embodied peace. It was clear she not only practiced yoga, but lived it. Laura emulated everything I needed in my life—peace, light, harmony, and acceptance. Laura was a personified version of what I wanted to be like once I was recovered.

Journal Entry on 3/2/14:

On Friday, 2/28/14, I had my second yoga lesson with Laura. We worked on breathing. She told me that as I get stronger/healthier, we would do harder poses. We talked about food. She was helping me to not be so afraid of food. When I met with her the first time, she asked me what I ate, and I told her. She was worried that I was having only three meals a day with a minor snack. So, on Friday she told me about many health snacks that she eats, too. Here they are: hummus, yogurt, peanut butter, nuts, cheese, almond butter, and eggs. She told me to try a new food, even if it is one single strand of spaghetti or one goldfish. So, yesterday, 3/1/14, I had a little hummus and veggies as a snack. Boy, was it good! I have missed hummus. Laura told me it is such a healthy snack. I was proud of myself, and my mom was, too. Laura also told me about other alternatives like having spaghetti squash instead of pasta. Or having whole wheat or gluten-free pizza dough. She is trying to help me eat "real food." I like that she is helping me. I trust her! I also like that she enjoys Whole Foods and Hannaford's, too! Laura also assured me that by having the serving size provided on the package, everything would be okay. The serving size is there to tell you a healthy serving and thus use it. Laura has and is helping me. I am so glad I found her! Laura even told her husband that she was so glad that we found each other.

I practiced yoga with Laura weekly over the month of March. Each practice started off with an encouraging meditation into relaxation, followed by a sequence of yoga postures. Warrior II made me feel strong and connected to the earth. Tree pose made me feel rooted to the ground. And child's pose allowed me to feel comfort. I danced through each yoga pose, feeling present. It was my one hour a week I could truly do something for myself and not be concerned about food. Although my time with Laura did not progress any longer than the four private yoga sessions, she opened the yoga gates for me and introduced me to the practice of stillness.

My yoga journey seemed to halt, rather abruptly, with my declining health. Physically, I was still standing, but mentally and emotionally I was depleted. Not only were people losing me, but I was losing myself. I felt stuck. Recovery was proving harder than I thought. Yoga was great for my mind, but it was not curing me. I wanted a magic spell to be cast over me to cure me from this horrible disease. My mom was scared. She could see my withering away, and she saw the pain I was in.

Letter from Mom:

Sara,

I miss you. I miss talking to you without the heaviness of your health hanging over our heads. I miss going out with you, whether it's to shop or have lunch. I miss looking at you and having you look back with life and excitement in your eyes. I miss seeing you happy and hearing you laugh. I miss seeing you healthy. I miss you not being cold or tired. I miss talking to you about school, friends, college, and life. I miss laughing with you. I miss laughing at Daddy with you! I miss you being healthy. I love you... any way or any size. I love you whether you earn an A or a C. I love you when you're angry at me. I love you. I love you. I want you to be happy and healthy. I will do anything in the world to keep you healthy. I will stand on my head or scream from the top of a mountain if that's what it takes. I will always support you. I will never leave you. I will always take care of you because that's what mothers do. It's what you will do for your children. I love you. I LOVE YOU!

Chapter Six

"You can handle anything, even the things you think you can't handle. You are a lot stronger and wiser than you understand right now. You are capable of getting past your worst days."

—EMILY MAROUTIAN

April 4, 2014

As the seasons began to change, the bitter warmth of April set in. The winter snow melted, and early signs of spring were underway. The sun's appearance, if only for a few hours throughout the day, sent hope that maybe there was truly a light at the end of this grueling tunnel. That hope seemed to shed mercy on itself at what became my last appointment with Dr. O'Brien.

At that appointment, Dr. O'Brien told me she was taking a medical leave of absence. She tried to sell me on the idea that the pediatrician who was covering was a wonderful, kind, and nurturing doctor. She also tried to reassure me that all the details concerning my health and recovery plan had been relayed to the new doctor, Dr. Coakley. It did not phase me that I would have a new doctor for the interim. In some ways, I was so tired of Dr. O'Brien that a new person seemed promising. As long as Dr. Coakley knew I did not want to be hospitalized and I wanted to continue to work on recovery at home, I did not care Dr. O'Brien was leaving. People were coming in and out of my life all the time. I was immune to loss.

I had my first appointment with Dr. Coakley scheduled for Friday at 2:30 p.m. A few days before the appointment, my mom received a call from the doctor's office, moving the appointment. The new appointment time of 5:30 p.m. seemed odd at first, but perhaps Dr. Coakley wanted to spend more time with me and not feel rushed to transition to another patient.

By the time 5:30 p.m. rolled around that Friday, the sky was dark. Although there were sprinkles of stars, my eyes were blinded by streetlamps and headlights. When we arrived at the doctor's office, the nature of the environment felt sparse. The office staff had left for the day, the waiting room was empty, and the after-hours cleaning team had already arrived. My mom and I looked at one another and then around the room, unsure of what to do. The waiting area was quiet, and every minute sound was audible. The approach of footsteps created a feeling of relief, knowing that we could get the appointment moving.

"Sara, I can take you back," said the nurse, my mom following.

The nurse went through the motions like she always did, recording my height and weight, checking my heart rate, and taking my blood pressure. It was a monotonous routine. She did not ask me questions or wonder how my week was. She merely did her job and left. It was cold and sterile. Shortly after there was a knock at the door and Dr. Coakley appeared. She was all business dressed in black slacks and a form-fitting blouse. Her hair was short and curly, and her small stature made it seem like a poke to her shoulder would send her tipping over. I felt my heart beat faster. I looked down at my fingernails as I nervously picked away at my cuticles. She made me feel intimidated as she walked in, her face expressionless and her mood cold.

Without any introductions or a warm welcome, Dr. Coakley sat down and said, "I think it is time for you to go to a hospital program." The words seemed to flow out of her mouth easily and calmy. There was no emotional depth. Her words appeared rehearsed and premeditated. I felt my brain shatter into a million different emotions. I had an immediate urge to run out of the room and slam the door shut. I wanted to fall into my mom's arms and scream, *Why is this happening to me?*

Tears began to stream down my face, as I grabbed hold of my head, shaking it in both disbelief and frustration. "No. No. No. No, please no. I can't go. No," I sobbed.

"What do you mean?" my mom asked.

Dr. Coakley handed me a box of Kleenex. "You are very sick, Sara. You need help. You need to get better. I think you should go home and pack a bag."

I tried to hide my face, covering my hands over my eyes, as I sniffled and licked away tears. "You can go out the back door if you would like," Dr. Coakley said.

She was short and ruthless. She was cold and apathetic. She was cruel and merciless. The conversation felt inhumane. If a child diagnosed with cancer needed to be hospitalized, is that how they would have been told? What was Dr. Coakley thinking? Had Dr. O'Brien not had a conversation with her? Did she not want to treat me?

As tears fogged my eyes blurring my vision, my mom stood next to me looking helpless and confused. Dr. Coakley had gone in for the jugular without a care in the world. Was going to the hospital what she thought would be a quick fix? I did not need a professional to try and shove peanut butter down my throat or give me some absurd diet regimen or send me to the hospital. I needed a someone to throw me a life raft and stick with it, not hold it against me, threaten me, or tell me some pity story about people dying from this disease. I needed empathy and consistent care and the reassurance that my team would support me through this deadly disease.

That was my last appointment with any doctor at that practice. We never stepped foot back in the office again. We lost trust in the practice and the doctors. How could someone go to school for so long and spend so much time learning about the human body and not know a thing about social skills? The experience continued to reaffirm that doctors did not know how to treat my disorder. They wanted to cure it physically, but they did not realize it was a mental disease, and it was my mind that needed help.

As my mom and I got into the car that evening, she took my face into her chest and gave me a long and powerful kiss. "I love you baby girl," she said. Tears streamed down my cheeks, creating a moist and sticky feeling beneath the creases of my neck. There were flakes of damp tissue on my mouth, as I wiped away the tears.

The car ride felt long and exhausting, as we headed to the hospital. Despite my pleading to not go and my mom's confusion as to how and why this was all happening, we went. When we arrived at the emergency room, the lights from the entrance of the hospital woke me. I slowly opened my eyes, adjusting to the brightness against the darkness of the sky. I struggled to get out of the car, still half asleep, my legs wobbling. As we walked into the emergency room, I was brought back to a room as though the hospital knew I was coming. We later found out Dr.

Coakley called the hospital to inform them that I was coming. My parents were held hostage at the check-in desk having to answer a myriad of insurance questions.

The nurse instructed me to put a hospital gown on and lay down on the bed. I felt as though I was in a daze. A symphony filled my ears of people shuffling in and out of the hallway. I sat there following the movements of the nurses. I played with the string on the gown, rolling it up and then unrolling it, counting how many times I could roll it until it could not be rolled anymore. The nurse walked back in, wheeling a machine, and holding a box of wires. "This is going to monitor your heart rate, sweetie. The machine makes funny sounds, but don't worry about that," she said. She peeled off the plastic piece of each sticker and stuck them one by one onto my chest. *Beep.* She turned on the machine, red and white lines appearing on the screen. "I will be back in a few minutes to check on you," she said.

I nodded. My eyes darted from the machine to the stickers on my chest. I knew if I breathed faster, the number would get higher. So, I did just that. My heart felt like it was about to cross the finish line at a marathon. I kept telling myself to breathe faster. Breathing faster meant my heart rate would increase. And, if my heart rate reached a normal rhythm, I didn't need to be here. I kept telling myself, *Just breathe faster, Sara. Breathe faster. That is your way out.*

While I lay on the bed watching the numbers on the screen, I took inventory of my surroundings. My mom and dad had finally made their way to the room and were sitting on the two chairs in the far-right corner. Next to them was a hand-washing station and the only thing separating me from the emergency room was a flimsy curtain. As I continued to look around, I felt an insatiable hunger that I had not felt before. Maybe it was all the energy I was using from breathing, or maybe it was the hell Dr. Coakley put me through, or perhaps it was me unconsciously trying to prove that I could eat and did not need to be at the hospital. Whatever perpetuated my hunger, I could not satiate it with my saliva and the smell of the alcohol-scented air only made me want to fill my nose with something more satisfying.

I looked over at my mom so she could see my face and said, "Mom, I'm hungry. I want to go home and have dinner." "Sara, what do you want me to do? Dad can get you something in the cafeteria. I don't know if you will like anything though," my mom replied. I shrugged and frowned, my eyebrows furrowing, "Fine. I'll have something from the cafeteria. What can I have?" My mom, looking surprised, said, "You can have anything you want honey. Do you want dad to see if they have any yogurt?" "Sure," I said.

A few minutes later, my dad appeared, a yogurt parfait in hand. I felt an initial wave of panic. Why had I agreed to eat it this? What was I doing? Why did I commit to eating such a foreign food? He handed me the cup and a spoon. I unwrapped the spoon, slowly peeling away the plastic and inspecting it, making sure he did not contaminate it. I dipped the spoon in the yogurt and mixed the berries. I felt my parents' eyes on me. The pressure was on. I ate the yogurt, one spoonful at a time, without mentally thinking about it. I was determined to do anything to get me out of the hospital. Just as I set the empty cup down on the table beside me, the doctor walked in.

Doctor: "Hello, Sara. How are you?"

Me: "Fine."

Doctor: (Washing his hands and putting gloves on.) "Can I take a listen to your heart?"

Me: (Nodding.)

Doctor: (Looking from me to my parents.) "I think it would be a good idea for you to stay at the hospital. Your heart rate was pretty low when you came in."

Me: "No. No. No. Please no."

Mom and Dad: (Blank stares.)

Me: (Looking at my mom.) "I will eat more. I promise. I will eat more."

Mom: "Can we have a few minutes to think about this?"

Doctor: "Yes, of course. I will come back in ten minutes." (Doctor left.)

My mom buried her face in the palm of her hands, looking helpless. "Sara, we cannot let you live like this," she cried. I aggressively stroked my hands through my hair, fear filling my body. "No, please no. You can't make me stay. Take me home. Please." My dad stood there silent. "Sara, if we take you home, you have to eat more. You have to promise us you will," my mom said. "I promise," I pleaded.

My eyes focused on my mom. She sat, full of overwhelm, sadness resorting over her face. My dad, emotionally stoic, stood upright. Despite the ensemble of beeping, sirens, and crying babies, the room felt silent. I looked at my parents and pleaded, my glassy eyes trying to convince them that I would eat more. A knock at the door broke us out of our trance.

Doctor: "Do you mind if I come in?"

Mom: "Yes, of course. Please come in."

(Everyone looking at one another.)

Mom: (Crying.) "We are going to take Sara home tonight."

Doctor: (Nodding.)

Mom: "Is there anything we need to do?"

Doctor: "I will have the nurse print out the paperwork for you to sign, saying that you are taking Sara home. Sara, please know you are welcome back anytime to get help."

Me: (Nodding.)

My parents' desire to make me happy contradicted what my body truly needed in that moment. They chose to bring me home that night.

Letter from my mom:

They wanted to admit you and I said no. Looking back, that is one of the most absurd things I have ever done. Can you imagine an ER doctor wanting to admit you because you were so sick, and I said no. Your mother said no. You promised that night that things would get better, that you would eat more, you promised me. But your illness was too strong. This was killing you.

April 8, 2014

Voicemail Message from Dr. Reed to my mom, in the morning:

Hi Stacey. My name is Dr. Reed. I am the medical director for the Inpatient Eating Disorder Center. I think Sara would benefit from our program. Please give me a call back at a convenient time.

It was just another day at school. When the bell rang at 1:40 p.m., I shuffled down the hallway, exchanged my binders for textbooks, and put my coat on. As I walked out the side door,

I saw my mom's white Murano in the distance. I got in the car and put on my seat belt. My mom was quiet. She barely made eye contact with me. As we drove away, I could tell something was wrong, but I did not know what. Attempting to break the silence, I said, 'I really don't like my math teacher. She doesn't explain anything."

"Mhm," my mom replied.

"I need to stay after for her class tomorrow. I have a test on Friday."

She focused on the road. Her green eyes, usually filled with empathy and compassion, never graced me with their presence. Her warm hands and soft fingers never caressed my arm. She simply drove.

When we got home, I walked into the kitchen and put my backpack on the chair. As I heard the shuffling of my dad's feet coming up the stairs, I felt my body become cold. My heart beat faster, and I could feel his presence hovering. My hands quickly fumbled around in my backpack, searching for a folder, trying to hide my face. "Sara, we need to talk to you," he said, leaning against the counter, my mom still in the doorway. "No!" I said, my feet moving faster than my mouth. I ran upstairs, slamming my bedroom door shut. I curled up in a fetal position, my hands covering my eyes. I knew what was happening. "Sara, you need to go to the hospital," my dad said, now standing in my bedroom. I started screaming. "No! You're liars. You said you wouldn't send me to the hospital. I hate you!" I flailed my body against the floor, creating a rug burn beneath my feet. "Sara, you are so frail. We need to help you," my mom cried, as she stood in the doorway. I continued wailing, tears sweating the palms of my hands. "No! Please no, Mummy. Please no. Don't do this to me."

My face was an ocean of tears. I felt confused, frustrated, mad, angry, and sad. I was helpless. Having to go to the hospital was proof that I was failing. I could not beat this disorder. I wanted to be done. I wanted to quit. I placed my hands around my neck, pushing my fingers in, taking a deep breath through my mouth, hoping, and praying somehow, I could make this all stop. "I will kill myself!" I screamed.

My dad stood against the dresser, tall and distant, scratching his forehead, as though he was looking for a solution. My mom, keeping a safe distance between the situation and her emotions, remained in the doorway. Resentment clouded my body. I hated them. I hated my mom for not stopping me. I hated my dad for not showing any emotion. And I hated myself for trusting anyone. I wanted to die. I did not want to fight anymore. I did not want to live anymore. I wanted to be done. My mind and body needed a break. I needed a permanent break.

Unexpectedly, my dad, frustrated with sadness and guilt, picked me up. I did not scream or yell. My hands broke away from my neck, the tears paused, and I surrendered. My body took over and my mind lay to rest. My screaming had dissipated. I knew I had lost control over the situation and there was no more negotiating or bargaining. The decision had been made. I was being admitted to the hospital.

That night, I was admitted to the Adolescent Medical Floor at the hospital. When we arrived at the hospital, I was taken upstairs to the unit. The hallways were dark and quiet, and I was exhausted. I made my way from the hospital gurney to the bed, sitting cross-legged, scanning the room. A TV was attached to the bed and a pull-out chair was in the corner. A floor-to-ceiling window only let in darkness and a frigid draft. My mom, finally done completing paperwork, brought a sense of familiarity to this new and unanticipated environment. I felt the weight of my head begin to fall to my shoulder. My body craved sleep. My mom pulled the sheet up to my chin, fluffed my pillow, and kissed me on the forehead. "Goodnight, my love. Get some rest."

Beep. Beep. Beep. Beep. Beep. Beep. The sound of machines alarmed me the next morning, waking me up from a deep sleep. As I yawned, the sunlight created a shadow on the floor, adding warmth to the room. I squinted my eyes, my sight blurry. The clock read 7:30 a.m. "Did you get some sleep last night?" my mom asked, walking toward me.

"Yes," I said. I lifted my arms, ready to take a stretch. I felt the weight of something beneath me. I looked down and saw a small, plastic IV tube hanging off the inner crease of my elbow. I must have been too tired the night before to remember that the nurse took my blood. I pulled the covers off noticing the oversized hospital pants I was wearing and the grippy socks that warmed my feet. The room smelled like a hospital—antiseptic with an artificial fragrance and a hint of bitterness. As I stood up, almost tripping over my pants, I realized the sink was taped off. There were layers of tape wrapped over the faucet. Odd, I thought. There were no mirrors and as I fumbled over to the bathroom, the door was locked. I looked over at my mom and said, "I need to go to the bathroom. What do I do?"

My mom flagged down a nurse and when the nurse arrived, she informed me of the bathroom protocol. "The door must be propped open. You pee in bowl, and be quick."

I looked at my mom quizzically. Why did the door need to be open and why did I need to pee in a bowl? As I walked in, I saw a sitz-like bowl in the toilet. I pulled down my pants and maneuvered my body, but there was no comfortable way to sit. Squatting would have to do. As I pulled up my pants and reached my hand over the knob to flush, the nurse barged in. "I will do that!" She shooed me to my bed. Why couldn't I flush the toilet? I was embarrassed and degraded. The rigidity around going to the bathroom felt like an invasion of my privacy.

After the nurse finished in the bathroom she said, "In a few minutes, Renee, the Certified Nursing Assistance, will take you to breakfast. Today, your breakfast has been chosen for you because you arrived here late last night. Moving forward, you will get to choose your meals based off the menu." A few minutes later, there was a knock at the door.

Renee: "Hi, Sara. My name is Renee. I am going to be taking you to breakfast today."

Me: "Okay."

Renee: "I need to grab you a wheelchair first, honey. Let me find one."

Me: (Looking at my mom.) "Why do I need a wheelchair?"

Mom: "I'm not sure."

Renee: "Here we go! I found one. You can come and take a seat honey."

Mom: "Um, why does she need a wheelchair?"

Renee: "That's what was on her chart this morning. I can check again with the nurse. Usually, they have patients in a wheelchair if their weight is too low to walk."

Mom: (Confused.) "Um, okay. Just sit in the wheelchair, Sara, and I will talk to the doctor."

Renee walked me to a conference room with a long wooden table. There was a tray piled with food. She wheeled me to the chair and said, "All right, Sara. Here is your breakfast. Now, they want you to eat everything off the tray. If you don't eat something, they will give you Ensure to supplement." I felt overwhelmed. There were eggs piled on one another and Texas-style toast painted in butter. The carton of milk taunted me, and the cereal seemed like more than enough. I poured the milk into the bowl of cereal, hoping I could kill two birds with one stone. As I spooned each bite of cereal into my mouth, Renee said, "Also, you have thirty minutes to eat. I will set a timer. Whatever you don't finish, they will give you an Ensure."

I rolled my eyes and focused on eating. I chewed each forkful of egg, drank sips of milk, and swallowed every bite. I did not think about what I was eating. Instead, I merely went through the motions. It was easier that way. I treated it like a test, and I needed to get an A. When I finished and pushed the tray away from me, Renee shook the milk carton and spooned the crumbs of cereal to the side of the bowl. "Drink that last bit of milk and eat those crumbs," she said.

After breakfast, Renee wheeled me back to my room. "Also, just to let you know. You cannot use the bathroom thirty minutes after any meal. Make sure if you need to go to the bathroom, you go before eating," she said as she left the room.

It took me some time to understand the rules on the unit. They did not trust me. They merely assumed I'd attempt to purge or hurt myself, which was why they were territorial around bathroom usage and why the sink was taped off. Timers were set during meals, so I did not spend too much time in front of food. Ensure was a threat to force me to eat. And the wheelchair was a punishment, despite me eating everything in front of me. I felt dehumanized. I was being treated as though I truly had befriended my eating disorder. I wanted, just as badly as my family and the doctors, to get better. But I was so afraid of food. It was terrifying.

I settled in my room that morning, changing from one T-shirt to another. I sat back on the bed, ready to put the TV on, and take a nap. There was a knock at the door and my mom, dad, and I looked at one another, wondering what was coming next. The medical director and her team entered my room and there was a distinct energy that came with them. It was stiff and uninviting. Dr. Reed, dressed in a blue, four-button cardigan with her blonde hair slicked back in a bun, stood tall and narrow. Nurse Hayes, who wore black pants and a sweater, stood stout and unwelcoming. Jill, the dietician, and Lisa, the social worker, trailed behind. The four women stood in a military line, with haphazard smiles.

Dr. Reed came toward me, reaching out her hand. I hesitantly reached out mine, unsure if I wanted to accept her welcome. I wanted to know about her. I wanted to know if she ate whatever she wanted when she wanted. How easy was it for her to eat? Did she truly understand what I was going through? Perhaps she sensed my uncertainty because as my mind began questioning her motives, I felt her hand on mine. Her fingers sent a chill throughout my body.

Dr. Reed: "It's nice to meet you, Sara. I spoke to your mom yesterday on the phone, and I was really worried about you. I'm really glad you're here. We want to help you. I am going to write all our names on the whiteboard behind me because I can imagine it will feel hard to remember all of us. While I write our names, I'm going to have everyone introduce themselves. Nurse Hayes, why don't you go first."

Nurse Hayes: "Good Morning. My name is Nurse Hayes. I am here almost every day. It's nice to meet you all."

Dr. Reed: "Jill, why don't you go next."

Jill: "Hi Sara! My name is Jill, and I am the dietician on the unit. I will work on your meal plans while you're here."

Dr. Reed: "Great, and Lisa, why don't you go."

Lisa: "Hi, Stacey and Michael. I am the social worker on the unit and will be working with you both while Sara is here."

Mom: (Staring motionless.)

Dad: (Staring motionless.)

Me: (Staring motionless.)

Dr. Reed: "We will meet with you as a team once a week. I

will come to check in on you almost daily. There is a psychologist who will meet with you, Sara, at some point today or tomorrow. If you need anything, please don't hesitate to ask the nurses on the unit. We are here to support you."

Mom: "Thank you."

Dad: "Thank you."

Me: (Blank stare.)

It felt like an audition. We all knew why I was there. It was not some crazy secret. I had an eating disorder. Instead of making small talk, exchanging introductions, and beating around the bush, they could have just cut right to the chase. I was sick and I was there to get help. I was not there to make friends or have some grand epiphany that recovery was the best thing ever. I was at the hospital because I needed to be not because I wanted to. And, for that reason, I was not going to recover on the unit. I knew my only way out was to ace the test, and that's what I was going to do. My mind was set.

Once the team left, my parents and I sat staring at one another. My mom looked at me and said, "Sara, I am going to go home for a little while and shower."

I nodded, fighting back the tears. "Okay," I said. "Can dad stay here with me?"

My mom looked at me and then turned her head to my dad. My dad and I had not been on good terms. We avoided one another and allowed our stubbornness to impact our relationship. But that appeared to change when I went to the hospital. My dad walked over to me, and we hugged, our first embrace in months. I needed him and he needed me. We needed each other. I cried on his shoulder, dampening his shirt. "I love you, Sara," he said.

My parents came every day to the hospital and stayed from dawn until dusk. They rotated every hour sitting in the stiff and uncomfortable hospital chair, eating bland deli sandwiches from the cafeteria, and breathing in stuffy hospital air. As each hour went by, the days seemed to blend into one another. I followed the same tedious routine:

6:00 a.m.   Nurse wakes me up and prods me with a needle to take my blood

6:30 a.m.   Brush teeth and change into a different t-shirt

7:00 a.m.   Dietician technician takes my meal orders for the day

7:30 a.m.   Bathroom (because I can't pee after breakfast for 30 minutes)

8:30 a.m.   Breakfast

9:00 a.m.   TV

10:00 a.m. Bathroom (because I can't pee after snack for 30 minutes)

10:30 a.m. Snack

11:00 a.m. More TV

11:30 a.m. Bathroom (because I can't pee after lunch for 30 minutes)

12:00 p.m. Lunch

12:30 p.m. Games with Dad

2:30 p.m. Bathroom (because I can't pee after snack for 30 minutes)

3:00 p.m. Snack

3:30 p.m. More games and TV

4:30 p.m. Bathroom (because I can't pee after dinner for 30 minutes)

5:00 p.m. Dinner

5:30 p.m. TV

6:30 p.m. Said goodbye to parents for night

7:00 p.m. TV

7:30 p.m.   Bathroom (because I can't pee after snack for 30 minutes)

8:00 p.m.   Snack

8:30 p.m.   Bed

My anxiety continued to grow as the impending question around when I would be discharged consumed me. I was eating everything I was told, and I was following the rules. And most importantly, I was passing all the *tests*. I wanted to be home. As it was with everyone else, my physical disorder was being treated, but not my mental disease.

After ten long and grueling days, I was finally discharged. Although it was a celebratory moment, I felt discouraged and scared. There was no way my mom was going to be able to take control at home like the hospital was able to do. They were two vastly different environments. The hospital was a safe place that maintained authority. The doctors determined all my decisions, including when, where, and what I was going to eat and how I was going to fill my time. I did not have to worry about school or grades. There was no fighting with my parents. In some ways, having no control eased me. There were no expectations other than to eat. And although that was an extremely challenging expectation, the motivation to do anything to get out of the hospital fueled me. What was going to fuel me when I left?

Although I had gained some weight in the hospital, I left just as mentally and emotionally depleted as when I was admitted. I felt neutral about the weight gain and in some ways this perpetuated thoughts of encouragement that I could perhaps do it at home. I questioned whether going home was the right thing to do. As much as I was challenged in the hospital, it was a safe space. There were no openings at outpatient settings, so going to another program was not an option. But going back to the very environment that I developed my disorder in seemed counterproductive. And for that reason, I was unable to maintain any weight gain at home. I continued to lose weight.

Letter from my mom years later:

Sara,

I've often referred to anorexia as a "dirty disease." Physicians treat patients with eating disorders extremely poorly. They would never treat a child with cancer or diabetes or a broken arm the way they treated you. There always seemed to be a sense of aggression and harshness when medical personnel spoke to you. They weren't helping, they were being mean, which just reinforced your distrust for any doctor who was trying to help you. No one smiled or tried to build trust or showed any compassion.

It was an awful circle of mistrust. You didn't trust the medical staff and they didn't trust you. I wanted to trust you but wasn't sure, and I wanted to trust the medical staff but wasn't sure.

The immediate outcome of your hospital stay was that you gained some weight. You followed their rules and ate what they told you to eat, and you did gain some, albeit a small amount of weight. I believed that the hospital would change things, that somehow you would walk out the door and no longer have an ED anymore. But that was not the case, and no sooner than we got home were things back to "normal." I thought that the hospital was going to be the "golden ticket" and you would get your life back, we would get our lives back. It really just compounded the situation by leading to more appointments and more stress. I think it was about 5 months later, around fall of 2014, that we stopped seeing the doctors affiliated with the hospital. So, the question of how things changed in the hospital is that they really didn't, other than that it reinforced how sick you were, how much power this had over you, and how scared I was for you.

As far as my experience, I felt judged as a mother. I felt inadequate, and I felt I had failed you. I did fail you. It was devastating, beyond devastating, to see you in the hospital knowing that you were missing out on life. I remember asking you if you wanted me to bring your phone and you said something like no, no one's going to text me, or no one is going to know I'm not in school. I couldn't imagine that. Your phone was on your bedroom nightstand, and I picked it up and saw that no one had texted you. My heart broke.

Mom

Chapter Seven

"*Though no one can go back and make a new start, anyone can start from now and make a brand new end.*"

—CARL BARD

April 2014 Cont.

An eating disorder is like a fly. It is a fly that keeps buzzing around you. It is that fly that makes circles around your head, preventing you from keeping flowers on your kitchen counter and goes after your juicy burger every time you are about to take a bite. It is that fly you keep swatting away and no matter how many fly traps you set up, the amount of money you spend on expensive organic products, or the time you devote on Pinterest looking up concoctions, it will not go away. That fly is always there, from the moment you wake up to the moment you go to bed. And maybe, just maybe, while you are sleeping, you find some relief and you start to realize that if you ignore the fly for long enough, you might just forget it is even there. That is, until you do something that triggers it. That fly, that damn annoying fly, was my eating disorder. The more I ignored it, the more difficult it became to deal with.

I returned to school the following Monday. My mom and I sat in the conference room in the principal's office waiting for my re-entry meeting. My mom was sitting to my left, the nurse to my right, and the school psychologist was sitting across from me. Because there were no windows, the room was thick and damp. As we sat there, the school psychologist was on her phone and the nurse was typing on her computer. It felt as though everyone had something better to do than spend their first hour at work at this meeting. And although the meeting was about me and for me, I still felt small and unimportant.

Just as I was about to pass time by picking my cuticles, Mrs. Smiley, my guidance counselor, walked in. She was a petite woman, with short, brown hair that angled her face. Her smile broke the unannounced discomfort in the room. "Good morning, Sara, we are glad to have you back," she said. I peered at her while keeping my head down and nodded. Once she sat down, the nurse gave a speech, which she might as well have handed out lyrics for because everything she said felt scripted. I had only been out for a week and a half. I did not understand why I needed a re-meeting. I understood it was protocol, but I was not suicidal or grieving the loss of a family member. There was nothing they could offer me that would help.

I was eager to get to class, and after the nurse ended, I felt a sudden glimpse of hope that I could return to my routine. But just as the nurse wrapped up, the psychologist chimed in, "And if you ever need anything, feel free to come to my office. I have plenty of stress balls and fidgets." I was confused. I had never met her before and did not even know where her office was in the school. What was a stress ball going to do for me? I had an eating disorder. I could not—or would not—eat. A stress ball was not going to fix that.

After the meeting ended, I quickly grabbed my backpack and walked to class. By the time I got to class, the period was already halfway over. After being out for a week and a half, the last thing I wanted was to walk into class late with all eyes on me. As I stood in front of the classroom door, my hand hesitated to turn the knob. I debated turning around and sitting in the library until the next period. But as I contemplated, I noticed my hand was already turning the knob and before I knew it, I was walking into the classroom.

I was right. All eyes were on me. My Spanish teacher was standing at the front of the classroom. As I walked to my seat, I could feel people's eyes following me. No one said hello or even smiled. Everyone just stared and then the teacher carried on with her lesson as I slumped back in my chair.

That was how my first day back went. There was no, "Oh, Sara, you are back! How are you doing? Is everything okay?" My teachers treated me just as they had before I left. I did not receive any special treatment other than some extra time to make up missed assignments. It was not that I expected or even wanted a warm welcome, but a check in would have gone a long way.

During the last two months of my junior year, things did not change. I stopped eating again. I lost weight again. I was still afraid of food. It felt easier to remain in the world I was so familiar with than to change. The anxiety, pain, and guilt of trying to eat was overbearing. Those feelings compounded with weekly follow-up appointments with Dr. Reed continued to antagonize my feelings of resentment and frustration.

After my discharge, I was summoned to the outpatient clinic. The clinic was in a medical building that was tall and gray, and from afar, it looked vacant and neglected. The parking lot was ghostly, and walking through the institutionalized hallways on the creaky floorboards created an informal and musty atmosphere. Upon entering the clinic, the yellow walls were lined with pamphlets. Two women sat behind a shield of glass, their stone-cold gazes speaking louder than words. They always asked for my name and date of birth as my mom and I approached. Then they handed us a pile of paperwork, my mom's signature becoming more obscure as each consent form passed.

My name would eventually be called, late as usual, and I would repeat the same drill I had at Dr. O'Brien's office. *Take your shoes off and strip yourself down. Don't forget to take off your earrings; they might add extra weight [insert eye roll]. Turn around and step on the scale.* Even though I had been completing the same monotonous routine for the last year, I still felt like my dignity and rights to my body were being taken advantage of. Taking off my clothes and putting a gown on my bare skin felt shameful. I hated my body enough, taking off my clothes only made it worse.

I went for follow-up appointments for the last month and a half of school following my discharge. Things changed, however, at my appointment in mid-June. Instead of Dr. Reed calling me back, it was a medical student. She was a stout woman and short in stature. Her teeth were crooked, and her face was shiny, sweat filling the crevices of her neck. "Sara, I can take you back," she said. I looked skeptically at my mom. Should I go back? Where was Dr. Reed? Why was someone different meeting with me?

"Sara, go ahead honey. It's okay," my mom said.

I stood up and followed the medical student back. "How are you doing today?" she asked. "Good," I replied. She had me step on the scale and then follow her to the exam room.

As I sat on the exam table, still uncertain where Dr. Reed was, I continued to answer her questions. "Are you done with school?" she asked. "Yes," I said. "What are your plans for this summer?" she asked. "I am going on a school trip to Europe. I signed up for my high school's world travel club when I was a sophomore. It was before I got sick." "Oh. Hmm. How is that going to work?" she asked, in what felt like she was challenging me.

Initially, I thought she was referring to the details of the trip and the places we were visiting. "We are flying into England and spending a few days in different cities. There are teachers from my school going and some of my friends are also signed up. I know it will be hard to eat, but I am excited, and I think I can do it."

She stared at me, seemingly fixated on my last sentence. I was unsure what answer she was looking for but clearly the one I gave was not it. She did not say anything else, and instead, she picked up her clipboard, wrapped the stethoscope around her neck, and said, "I will be right back."

A few minutes later, Dr. Reed walked in, my mom following behind. Dr. Reed stood in front of me, with a threatening demeanor. She looked at me and said, "I do not think going on the trip is a good idea. It is too much walking, and it will not work." I did not know whether to cry, scream, or walk out of the room. So much of my life had already been taken away from me, and I was not going to let my disorder continue to vacuum up more.

My mom, sitting on the chair, looked paralyzed in surprise. I turned my head to face her, hoping to convince her through my eyes that I was going. And, similarly to when my mom and dad chose not to admit me to the hospital originally, my mom declined to respect Dr. Reed's indirect order. I lost friends, family members, and parts of myself over the last year. I was not ready to go through another year losing more. The trip was mine. I owned it. It was something I committed to long before my disorder and, as nervous as I was about the trip, I thought maybe it would be a chance for me to reclaim myself, even if it only lasted the ten days.

I felt like the medical student's question was a trap. Her "simple" question led to a monopoly of questions. If they wanted me to eat normally than why did they not want to let me experience normality? How much longer could I be confined to the bones of my body? Their discouraging and unsolicited suggestions continued to dehumanize me. I felt like an experiment, like someone you read about in medical studies. They wanted me to engage in weekly blood tests to help them decipher how calcium levels are impacted by anorexia. They suggested I join different groups and trial interventions. Despite how sick I was, I was so much more than my disorder. I was a person who was struggling. I was not an anorexic. I was someone struggling with anorexia.

My mom thanked Dr. Reed for her advice and said she would take it into consideration. The trip was paid for. I had been looking forward to it. And although it was perhaps another moment in which my parents' decision contradicted my health, they did not want to let me down.

That was my last appointment with Dr. Reed, which ultimately meant I had no providers. I was tired of doctors telling me how I could live my life and my parents were exhausted from being parented by doctors. We were done.

June 2014

Flight Attendant: "When the seat belt sign goes on, you must fasten your seat belt. Insert the metal fittings one into the other and tighten by pulling the loose end of the strap. To release your seatbelt, lift the upper portion of the buckle. We suggest you keep your seatbelt fastened throughout the flight, as we may experience turbulence."

Pilot: "Flight attendants, please prepare for take-off."

As I sat on the aisle seat of the plane, I looked around at my surroundings. I could feel the tightness in my chest, the tiredness in my legs, and the clenching of my jaw. I could not help but wonder how I was going to make it through the trip. I remember the poster I saw in the hallway that initially intrigued me. The Eiffel Tower stood tall and proud on the posterboard. The thought of traveling to London, France, and Germany over ten days seemed like a dream beyond belief.

Once I got sick, I lost touch with my emotions toward the trip. I did not have the mental capacity to think about it. In the month leading up to the trip, however, I felt as though I was traveling down a major highway, going a steady seventy-five when suddenly I come to a complete stop, traffic preventing me from moving forward. The traffic was my anxiety. What was I going to eat? What was I going to do if I did not feel well? As I considered my thoughts, a red light flashed, and a buzzing sound went off. My head was jolted to the side of the seat, and I realized the plane was taking off.

Just as quickly as the plane took off, we landed in London at Heathrow Airport. Upon landing, we raced off the plane, ready to take on the day. The teachers herded us through the airport and onto the bus to meet our tour guide. When we got to the hotel, I immediately called my mom. We talked for an hour. I felt drained. My body was tired, my mind was overwhelmed, and my heart hurt. It was not until that moment that I realized I was not physically at home and the impact of that realization was intense. What was I going to do if I did not want to eat what was served for dinner? My mom was not there to coach me or provide me an alternative. How was I going to survive?

Some days were better than others, while some merely sucked. I was not able to lick my lips of grease and leftover crumbs from fish n' chips or bite into warm, chocolate croissants. I did not chew my way through a fresh baguette or paint my teeth in warm brie cheese. I ate an apple, one apple, every day. That was all I was comfortable eating. Of course, I wished I could eat all the delicious food. At times, I vicariously ate through what my fellow peers were eating, imagining the various tastes permeating my palette. But every night on the phone, I told my parents that I ate all the foods everyone else was eating. I did not want to disappoint them, but most importantly, I did not want to worry them.

We walked for eight hours every day in the sweltering heat. We were free to eat lunch on our own and ate a sit-down dinner every night together. By the time dinner came, I had no energy left, not even enough to pick up my fork and attempt to eat, not that I would have eaten the food anyway.

I enjoyed the London Eye and the South Bank of the River Thames in London. I walked the 1,665 steps of the Eifel Tower and whether that was out of pure guilt for eating or my desire to experience the Eifel Tower, I was not sure. I put my toes in the sand at the beaches of Normandy and walked around various chocolate shops in Belgium, looking for homemade hot fudge to bring home.

As hard as the trip was for my mind, it was even harder for my body. The trip only perpetuated my body's decomposition. The energy I had went right to my brain to fight off feelings of frustration and anxiety. There was nothing left for my physical body. As a result, I was not mentally present for the trip. My memories faded and as each day passed, I hoped I would make it home safely in one piece.

When I returned home from the trip, I was even more malnourished than when I left. I conjured up false memories to reassure my parents I had a good time. It felt easier to provide skewed answers to questions my parents asked, rather than leave room for the imagination. I did not want to put pity on myself for not immersing myself in the European culture and dialect, so instead I answered questions with "good" and "okay" and worked to diverge conversations into different directions.

August 2014

After Europe, there was Virginia. My family had planned a trip to Virginia to reconnect with my paternal aunt and cousins. It was one of my last-ditch efforts at saving grace, or in my case, saving myself. I thought my sickness would instantly be cured by spending time with family that I had not seen in a while.

It was approximately a ten-hour drive to Virginia, and it was grueling. Each rest stop provoked an intensity of fear, anxiety, and angst. The smell of freshly baked Dunkin' Donuts mixed with sweet, herbed bread from Subway and oil from McDonald's French fries permeated the air at every rest stop. Those sweet and savory smells combined with the smells of burnt coffee, body odor, and restrooms reeking of urine sent a wave of nausea through my body. I was so far in my eating disorder that smells were just as triggering as the food itself.

The first time I put lotion on myself in over a year was when I was hospitalized. And the only reason I put lotion on my skin while I was in the hospital was because my skin was casually peeling apart. My fingers were raw, cracks patterned my hands. Before the hospital, I refused to use lotion. I did not put Chapstick on my lips, wear makeup, or even spray perfume on my body. I had an intense and irrational fear any tangible thing on my body would add weight. That was the extent of how far my eating disorder ruled my body.

With that mindset as my blueprint, each rest stop became more unbearable than the last. I was afraid the smell of greasy French fries would stain my clothes adding weight to my body. Afraid that somehow, the grease would find a way to enter my body, further weighing me down. And not only was it the smell of the rest stops that became debilitating, but it was also the fact that I could not or would not eat anything.

The trip, like Europe, became a blur over the years. There was one poignant moment, however, where I had a come-to-Jesus moment. One day, we were planning on going to a water park. I went into the bathroom in the hotel room to change into my bathing suit. It was a bathing suit that was about two years old and had likely seen better days. Starting with the bottoms, I put my right leg through and then my left. As I pulled the bottoms up and let go, they fell, blanketing my ankles. At first, I looked in the mirror and shrugged my shoulders, a bout of confidence kicking in. Hell yeah! You are getting thinner. Things still don't fit. Keep going! But as I put on the top and pulled it over my head, it was swimming over my chest. When I looked in the mirror again, I felt shame and sadness. What was happening to my body? Was the suit not fitting because I had lost so much weight? What was I doing?

I opened the bathroom door and called for my mom. She walked into the bathroom and looked at me in despair. It was not my face that gave it away, it was my body. "I don't know what to tell you Sara," she said.

Throughout the trip, we played our parts. My mom pretended to be annoyed at my dad for taking wrong turns on the road or snoring during the night. My dad jokingly ridiculed my mom about her lack of enjoyment at the beach. I masked my desire to be at home with laughs. We pretended to be a happy, loving, and fun family but, we were all exhausted. Not only exhausted of my disorder but exhausted by feelings of defeat. We were the personification of a bow a child attempts to tie on a present, just waiting to come undone by even the smallest amount of pressure.

September 2014

And just like that, summer turned to fall. As my mom and I drove home from our back-to-school shopping trip, I felt my head bob against the seat. As my eyes began to close, something in the distance caught my eye. Whether it was the red letters of Bertucci's that initially caught my attention or the fact that we were at a strip mall, something caught my attention. As we drove, getting closer to the trigger, I read the word *yoga* stamped against a small, brick building. My eyes homed in on the blue block letters. My mind began to reminisce about my first encounter with yoga when I met Laura. It felt like that was so long ago, and I craved being on my mat again. As I stared at the yoga sign like a hawk, my mom reached her hand over and tapped me on the shoulder, "Sara, are you okay?"

I turned to her and said, "Yeah, I'm fine. There's a yoga studio right there!"

When we arrived home, I propped myself on the couch, logged into my computer, and looked up the yoga studio's name. I scrolled through their class schedule and spotted a beginner class on Saturday's at 11 a.m. I knew yoga was good for my mental health and physical health. It felt like "safe" exercise, and I did not feel guilty for signing up. In my mind, it was not a rigorous workout that impacted my weight, but it also was a form of exercise and that felt empowering. Maybe I could eat more if I did yoga? I wanted to give it another try, so the following Saturday I found myself driving to the studio, turning into the parking lot, and pulling into a space.

The walls were painted a baby blue and the shades were pulled up, allowing sunlight to warm the room. I set out my mat, and I took in my surroundings. People slowly shuffled in, assuming their position in the studio. The teacher stood at the front of the room, his blue eyes saying hello to everyone. He looked at us and said, "Good morning, folks. Happy Saturday. Let's start in a seated position."

As he instructed us throughout the class, his warm and carefree sense of nature filled me with ease. He broke down the poses while cracking jokes, allowing beginners, like me, to feel confident and safe. When the class ended, I rolled up my yoga mat and put my shoes on. The teacher came over to me and asked how I felt. I responded, "I think I did great!"

Looking back at my response, it was far from the answer the teacher was likely asking. The teacher asked me how I was feeling, not how I thought I did. Of course I did great. In fact, everybody did great. But that was not what I was being asked. The teacher was asking me how I felt in my body. And at that exact moment, I could not answer the question. I was not attuned to my body. I was disconnected from it. But I continued to attend the weekly class for almost a year. It became part of my routine. It was my only sixty minutes of the week I did not think about food. Instead, I thought about myself. I took care of myself. I took care of my body. I began to learn what it meant to listen to my body.

Chapter Eight

"*I am loved and always have been loved and will always, always be loved. I have never been separated from this love, I have only convinced myself I was.*"

—GLENNON DOYLE

They say your biology becomes your biography. As a stickler for cleanliness and organization, a tenacity for independence and determination, and a magnet for anxiety and impatience, it felt inevitable that an eating disorder was in my future. I had everything going for me. I was the *perfect* person. It is no wonder I became afraid of the most vital resource the human body needs.

My rigidity, persistence, and drive were all ingredients I had on hand. Rigidity allowed me to follow strict measurement guidelines. Persistence got me through the hunger pains. And, drive, well, that got me to where I was… sick. But it turned into a battle, in which I added an extra cup of drive, another tablespoon of rigidity, and finished it off with a bag of persistence, underestimating the amount of flexibility and realism I had left. My reaction was not good. I lost the most innate ability the human body has—the desire to eat. It was too late to take out the extra ingredients. They were all so intertwined, already working their magic. It got to the point where my only option was to dump out the recipe and start over. Start over from scratch. I had to relearn how to eat.

Journal entry from November 1, 2014:

I think it's funny how a little over a year ago I started writing in this journal. I thought, at the time, I was ready to change. But let's be real, Sara, I was only fooling myself. I had no intention of getting better. I honestly imagined myself living with an eating disorder for the rest of my life. I mean, I know it will always be a part of me, but I truly pictured myself counting, restricting, and worrying about food for the rest of my life. I think I was so fearful of the hospital that I was willing to "try" and get better, but the problem was I didn't want to get better. I know now that I have to want to get better to change. So, maybe that's why I'm starting again. I am going to try journaling and reading the book. But who knows, it may not last long. So, here goes.

Mid-November 2014

I turned eighteen on November 4th, 2014. My parents and I huddled over the cake, sitting on the black, speckled granite countertop. Pink rosettes covered the snow, white buttercream and tall, hot-pink candles were perfectly placed in the center. My name was piped in light pink cursive frosting. Although the cake screamed joy and celebration, my face screamed pain and sadness. I was dressed in pink pajamas with polka dots all over. Not the big type of polka dots, the ones that were small and freckled. My chopstick thin legs swam in the pajama bottoms. My face was long and thin, looking disproportional to the rest of my body. My cheeks did not fill out like they normally had when I smiled. I looked tired, withdrawn, and unhappy. I took a big breath in and blew out the candles. My only wish was to make things go away.

What came over me once I turned eighteen, I will never know. Was I tired of living my life? Yes. Did I want to make changes? I think. Was my impatient self prepared for the journey? That's debatable.

A few weeks after my eighteenth birthday, as I sat on my bed, my zebra blanket covering my body, the *Real Housewives of New Jersey* playing in the background. I logged onto my computer, and I typed in the search bar "Blue Cross Blue Shield providers" and checked off the "dietician/nutrition" box. A list of providers appeared across the screen, pages and pages full. My eyes widened and my heart sank. How many providers was I going to have to filter through to find *the* one?

After exhausting the Blue Cross Blue Shield website, I turned to a simple Google search, *Nutritionists in Boston*. The name, Julie Starr-Wood, stared at me from the screen. I hovered the mouse over her name. Do I keep scrolling or do I click? I had already scanned through page after page of providers, each bringing me farther away from my goal. As my mind contemplated, my instinct took over. My right pointer finger pressed down on the mouse. The moment I blinked the screen changed. Her website was simple. A picture of her beautiful smile flashed across the screen, a short description about her, and a picture of her daughter sitting atop her back while doing a yogi plank. I knew she was *the* one. I clicked open a new tab, my fingers moving faster than my brain. I typed an email.

I said I was struggling with an eating disorder, and I was looking for help. A few days later, an email from her appeared in my inbox. Her response: "Sara, I would love to work with you. Let's set up a call." Sara, I would *love* to work with you. *Love* to work with you. I reread her words multiples times. I had lost everything over the last two years. My friends tossed me away like you throw a piece of gum out the car window. My extended family did not understand what was going on, and my relationship with my parents was a roller coaster. Julie wanted me. She wanted to work with me. She said she would *love* to work with me.

Late November 2014

I stepped into her office one day in late November. Her office was a yoga and barre studio. To the left was a white desk with barre socks sitting in a glass vase. Above the desk, a poster of Julie's beaming smile, with her long blonde locks hugging her face. Julie's smile greeted me ten steps before she did. She was wearing black lululemon leggings and an aqua blue tank top. She did not shake my hand. Instead, she hugged me. Actually, she squeezed me. How did she know I needed that? She walked me into the studio, and we sat down. The room was painted white and had floor-to-ceiling windows that allowed the sun in. I sat on a black bridge chair and a small table was placed between us.

Out of the corner of my eye I saw the scale. I felt my eyes wander from the scale to Julie. She caught me looking and said, "Well, let's get you on the scale." With the scale in front of me, I turned around. Her arm gently caressed my shoulder as she guided me on. I did not know what I weighed, and I felt okay with that. I felt safe. I did not need to worry about the number. Julie was there. She was going to help me. I believed that.

Our conversation flowed. I felt like I had known Julie for a lifetime. She empathized with me. She understood me. She got to know me on a personal level. She said, "You are not my patient, you are a client, and I work for you." She didn't treat me like I was some science experiment. She treated my eating disorder as a mental illness and something I needed help controlling.

There was no crazy food system like Tara had prescribed me, and she did not put the control in my parents' hands like the hospital did. She worked with me. She met me where I was at. She slowly pushed me, but not too hard. She never called me out when she knew I was failing her homework assignments. She knew my eating disorder was a pesky fly and despite my attempts to swat it away, it snuck up on me. She knew I was trying my best and some weeks, my best just got me by while other weeks my best opened new doors, doors that awakened my heart and made me feel alive again.

Each day presented a new challenge. Adding a third slice of turkey to a sandwich, switching from ninety-calorie wraps to bread, using whole milk instead of fat-free, trying larger portions of carbs, and working toward enjoying food was not an overnight success. Even though Julie was pushing me, just as Tara and the hospital had done, something was different. Maybe I was ready this time around. Maybe I trusted Julie. Or maybe I was finally ready to be free.

Journal entry on December 18, 2014:

I have finally found a nutritionist. Her name is Julie Starr-Wood. Her approach is so different and just liveable. I have accomplished a lot since I first saw her in December. However, right now I am at a standstill with my weight. It has stayed the same and I actually lost weight at my last appointment. Julie was telling me to eat things and I wasn't, plain and simple. I am in this constant battle with myself. I want to get better, but I am afraid. But I cannot pinpoint what I'm afraid of. Is it a fear of going back to the way I was, which I won't because I'm not that person anymore? Or is it because I'm afraid to look like someone else, which I won't because I'm me? Is it just a fear of gaining weight in general? I don't know. But I do know I need to overcome this.

It's hard because I trust Julie a lot. I'm still scared. It's something I must work on. I have been really sticking with Julie's suggestions and doing my best. I keep telling myself that a pair of double-zero jeans from Abercrombie and Fitch don't even fit me; they are too big. I mean Abercrombie, a double zero, doesn't fit! I'm eighteen years old. That is a problem! But this is where it's hard. When I try the clothes on, I feel sad and actually motivated to change, but when the time comes to eat, I get so worked up about putting three slices of turkey on a wrap. It's hard. That's why I give into the eating disorder some days because I don't want to contemplate with myself all day. But I know giving in just fuels the eating disorder, making it worse. So, that's why I've been working extra hard these last two weeks to improve and fuel the positivity. I don't want this to be my life.

I want to be a foodie, but in a positive light. I want to obsess over the prettiness of my food and not the caloric content. I want to go to restaurants and order the seasonal plate and not the salad. I want to enjoy food! I know that it's possible. I know I have determination, a lot of it. So, I will have to put it to the test. Here goes...

February 2015

Journal entry in February 2015:

As I made my wrap for lunch today, I realized putting on three slices of deli turkey did not send me into my normal panic. For about the last 2.5 weeks, I have been putting on three slices of deli with a piece of cheese. Surprisingly, I have not felt so nervous and anxiety ridden about it. I think I'm starting to take Julie's advice. I need to start looking around and seeing what other people's plates look like. Or, as Julie said, if she came to my house what and how much would I serve her? I mean, yes, the sandwich tastes better and is more satisfying. It's important to me that I don't just go through the motions this time around, but really dig deep and push myself. Just last week I had a chicken quesadilla for lunch. I even went out to the Neiman Marcus café and ordered something different from what I originally planned on getting. Julie is really trying to teach me how to eat all kinds of meals while still making sure all the good food groups are present. You know, sometimes I don't even go to yoga. This is good! It teaches me that shit happens, and things come up so you cannot always rely on the normal routine. The other day I had turkey sausage. I don't remember the last time I had that. I really have been expanding my palate both inside and outside the kitchen. I hope I can get through this.

Julie challenged me to try new foods. I always left my weekly appointments with Julie feeling motivated and confident that I could add in that extra slice of cheese on my sandwich, have those two scoops of rice at dinner, and put a handful of nuts into my cereal. There were days that I did add a spoonful of flax seeds to my raisin bran or an extra slice of cheese to my sandwich, but I usually took out the extra slice of cheese at lunch or short-changed myself by not eating pretzels. That was how my eating disorder played out. I was not necessarily lying to Julie because I had put the flax seeds on my cereal. But to ease me own anxiety, it felt safer if I refrained from a snack during the day. That cycle of wanting so desperately to free myself and try new things while keeping my disordered eating thoughts at bay was vicious and exhausting.

As I moved through that cycle, I continued to distract myself with school. Every morning, my mom dropped me off at 6:50 a.m. I made my way through the near-empty halls to my locker, exchanged my backpack for books, and walked to my first class. I watched the clock tick by, period after period. I ate lunch in the library alone every day. This was not only due to me not having friends to sit with, but the thought of the smell of frozen chicken nuggets burning in the oven coupled with the possibility of brushing my hand against a sticky table covered in hardened ketchup was enough to overwhelm me. I sat at the same computer in the far-right corner and ate. Once lunch was over, I knew I had one period left to go and, if I was lucky, I could go home after lunch if my last class was cancelled.

Amid school, disordered eating thoughts, and family chaos, there was college. Even though I was still just as mentally sick as I was when I first started seeing Julie, I was a typical senior, and I looked forward to life after high school. I applied to many schools, mostly in California: University of the Redlands tucked away in a homey town, midway between Los Angeles and Palm Springs; Sonoma State University in beautiful wine country; Russell Sage College in Troy, New York; Simmons College, an all-girls school in Boston, MA; and my number one choice, Whittier College, a small but academically rich school just outside of Los Angeles. I was and always had been a learner. There was no doubt in my mind that I would go to college and earn a degree.

Checking the mail became my only form of excitement. One afternoon, in early February, I drove up the driveway, my mom still at work and my dad traveling. I felt an urge to check the mailbox. As I walked to the mailbox, hugging my arms around my waist, the wind hitting my face, I wondered what piece of mail I would get from the hospital. Ever since I went to the hospital, they sent survey after survey, recruiting me to be part of yet another eating disorder study. I opened the mailbox and saw something peculiar. It was not a typical envelope. It was on the bigger side. It was yellow and purple. Hmm, I thought, probably another advertisement from Whittier College.

As I stepped inside, my foot halfway through the door, I slipped my finger underneath the sealed envelope. I pulled out a thickly folded piece of cardstock. Something seemed different. I walked over to the island, placing the rest of the mail on the counter, and unfolded the cardstock. It was more of an anxious opening as my finger began to tremble. As I opened it, I saw the word *congratulations* in white lettering. *Congratulations, Sara, on your early acceptance to Whittier College.* My mouth opened but no words came out. My heart felt full, yet it sank deeper within me. The part of me that was so eager to flee and make a new life for myself was contradicted by the daunting thought that maybe, just maybe, moving across the country was not actually in my best interest. But I quickly threw that thought to the back of my mind because this moment was the first time in a long time that I was happy, and I wanted to experience that emotion fully.

I needed to tell my mom! Should I call her? Should I wait until she got home? I decided to surprise her. I carefully folded the cardstock, placed it back in the envelope, and laid it on the counter. My mom got home around 4:30 p.m., and as she walked in the door looking exhausted and withdrawn, I jumped from the couch, and said, "Mom! I got something cool from Whittier. They are having some sort of tour that I think might be fun to do. Open the envelope and look."

I followed her to the counter, standing next to her, wrapped in a blanket. As she opened the cardstock, her facial expression became lighter. I watched as her eyes read every word, line by line. When she was done reading, she looked at me, put her arms around me, and gave me a hug. She kissed me on the top of my head. She was happy. I was happy. We were happy together, smiles cascading our faces, both of us hiding the deep pain within.

Life seemed okay. It was bearable. I called my dad. He was elated. It felt as though my acceptance brought us all closer together. It distracted our minds. It gave us something to look forward to. It gave us something to smile about.

A few weeks later, on a bitter cold day, clouds storming in the sky, we drove to Logan Airport to fly to California. As we toured Whittier College, the flowers were in full bloom and the sun shone bright in the sky warming my skin. I felt a glimmer of hope fill my body. I felt at home. I imagined myself underneath the tree, with its branches reaching out as if the tree were lending me a hand into my newfound happy place. I pictured myself sprawled out on a blanket, sunglasses atop my head, lying down, reading a book, drinking iced coffee, and laughing with friends. Everything about Whittier College felt right.

That night, while sitting on the bed in the hotel room, I looked at my mom and said, "This is it. I know Whittier is the one." She looked at me and smiled. But I could tell her smile was not truthful. Behind her smile was desperation and helplessness, a feeling of *How can I actually let my daughter to this when she is so sick?*

My mom asked me, "Sara, are you sure this is what you want?"

"Yes! You told me if I liked the school, you would put the deposit down after the tour," I said.

"Why don't we just wait until we get home, and I can do it then?"

"But you said you would."

"Okay, Sara," my mom replied.

May 2015

A few weeks leading up to my graduation, we took a trip into Boston. It was mid-May and despite the sun shining and people walking by in tank tops and shorts, I was dressed for winter, wearing a pink North Face fleece, jeans, and a sweater to protect my goosebump-covered arms. We walked along Newbury Street, heading toward the Lilly Pulitzer store. My dad propped himself on a nearby bench, legs crossed and phone in hand, as my mom and I poked around. I tried on a few dresses and some skirts, most falling off my body, blanketing the floor. Just as I lost hope in finding a perfect graduation dress, I put on a slim fitting blue and purple floral-patterned dress. As my mom pulled the delicate zipper up my back, I allowed my head to glance at the mirror. It fit. And not only that, but I loved it. It did not need altering. It did not need to be taken in on the sides. It did not need to be hemmed. It was perfect. As I walked out of the store, shopping bag in hand, I felt a sigh of relief.

Our next stop was lunch at a quaint restaurant with outdoor seating. Located in the heart of Back Bay, I had deemed it "safe" when I planned the day with Julie a week before. I already scoured the menu, making sure I found something I would eat, something that felt "safe." One that would not overwhelm my mind and send knots throughout my body. I ordered a Greek salad. I felt confident and somewhat excited as I waited for the food to arrive. I had done the researching and planning on what menu choices would satisfy both my stomach, but more importantly, my mind. But as I spotted the waitress coming over, I felt a wave of panic. As she arrived at our table, she dished out the fish n' chips to my dad and the hamburger to my mom. The moment the waitress put my salad down in front of me, my heart sank, and my chest became heavy. I could feel my cheeks became red and warm.

The dressing was on the salad. I tried to talk myself down. *Sara, it's okay. Just eat it. You will be fine.* But my frustration interfered. I asked specifically for dressing on the side. This was ridiculous. What was I going to do?

Although my mom, dad, and I did not verbally say what was wrong, we all felt it. "Sara are you okay?" my mom asked. "I don't know," I responded. "Do you want to send it back?" she asked again. "I don't know," I said.

My dad had already dug into his fish n' chips, tartar sauce and all. My mom began to dress her hamburger in ketchup as I stared—more like glared—down at my salad. I felt like a sand art bottle, all shaken up. Each color represented a different emotion. Red dominated the bottle, anger permeating my body. Gray sand, my anxiety, just like the red, rushing through. But there was a sprinkle of yellow, the hope inside me, still too small to step in. I felt mad yet eager. Sad yet determined. Anxious yet ready.

I excused myself from the table and went to the bathroom. I washed my hands in the sink, hesitant to look up at the mirror. I forced myself to look, to really look into my eyes. I saw desperation. I saw a girl who wanted so badly to just eat. I saw someone who was hungry, hungry enough to let go of the guilt, even just for a moment.

As I walked back to the table, I sat down, put my napkin on my lap, and picked up my fork. I did it. I ate the fucking salad. And that was it. While we ate, we talked about my graduation and things I needed for my dorm room in the fall. We talked like any other normal family. And I felt proud, proud of myself for eating the salad and proud of my parents for bearing with me.

June 2015

On Saturday June 15, 2015, I crossed the finish line. I had been running a marathon, turn after turn, the end barely visible in sight. When I finally saw the finish line, a crowd of people sitting in the distance, clapping their hands and smiles cascading their faces. I walked across the stage and graduated with my high school diploma. It was not only the day that I felt like I was free from high school, but a day in which I felt that much closer to being free of my eating disorder. As I sat on the stage looking out into the crowd, I saw people smiling and laughing, some even crying. I saw families hugging and patting one another on the back. I saw my parents, and for the first time in a long time, I saw them happy. I saw light in their eyes. A glow. I could feel how proud they were of me. How much they knew I had accomplished. But beneath that glimmer of happiness and light, I could see their uneasiness. Their hesitation. Their concern was palpable.

The moment I walked off the stage and into my parents' arms, I felt a sigh of relief and I know they did, too. The pressure of their hug warmed my body. We took pictures and laughed. We were that photogenic family you see on the paper photo when you buy a picture frame. We were so happy and carefree like life was simply perfect. But we knew there was a missing piece. I was still succumbing to my disorder. Anorexia was consuming my mental state. I still had not gained weight. I maintained my weight, but I had not truly counteracted my thoughts and utilized my yoga practice to become one with my body. I was still working toward a stable form of recovery. And that was scary, given the quick turnaround between graduation and college.

Chapter Nine

"Don't let anyone else pressure you into living a life you feel is not for you. Don't allow guilt or any other form of manipulation to throw you off your course. Your life is yours and you should live it the way you feel is right. Give yourself the permission you need to move forward in your own way."

—EMILY MAROUTIAN

September 2015

The day I moved into Whittier College is one that continues to remain clear in my mind. I sat at the table in the dining room of the hotel, eating some off-brand Special K cereal with one percent milk. My dad was preparing a meal set for a king: scrambled eggs, greased up bacon, and a bagel frosted with cream cheese. My mom sat down next to me, coffee in hand. I stared out the window next to me, gazing into the blue sky. I felt as though I were merely going through the motions, but I worked up an excited attitude and put on my mask. My mask resembled that of any typical freshman student moving into college on the first day—anxiety, nervousness, and excitement driving my actions. My mom looked over at me, put her hand on my shoulder, and asked, "Sara, are you ready to go?"

As I continued to stare off into the blue sky, I said, "No, let's wait ten more minutes." Maybe if I did not look at her as I said this, she would get the hint. The hint that maybe this was not the right move for me. Maybe, just maybe, she would say, "Sara, we are going home, all of us." Because maybe, just maybe, she knew I could not handle this.

My mom did not say those words, and I was too afraid to say them, too. The three of us got up, pushed our chairs in, and walked to the car. We loaded everything into the car the night before, which made our departure from the hotel quick. We rented a gray suburban, one of those gas guzzlers almost every Californian owns. As we drove to Whittier College, a twenty-minute drive from the hotel, I stared out the window. I caught glimpses of birds passing by, and I homed in on one bird. I so desperately wished to be that bird, free to move throughout the world, having the audacity, without shame, to do whatever I wanted, whenever I wanted. I would not have to consider how much money flights cost. I would not have to worry what others thought of me. I could travel from place to place until I was free of my eating disorder.

"Sara, we are here."

The sound of my mom's voice shook me out of my daydream and reality set in. I was not the bird, and I was never going to be that bird. I was here, in the car, at college, far from being free of my eating disorder.

Smiling faces lined the campus. Resident assistants stood out in their purple shirts, the color of Barney, directing new students and families. The campus is set on a cascade of green grass with modern and eccentric buildings. Clay tile roofing adorns the top of each building, giving it that Orange County, Southern California feel. Throughout the campus there are inlets of picnic tables and beautifully cared for trees that make it the perfect studying destination. The fields are well kept and sit at the far distance of the campus. Palm trees line the walkways, completing the look. My dad parked the car, and we made our way toward the crowd. I did my best to focus on each information table, but it was hard. My mind and body were preoccupied with the anxiety that was beginning to set in. *Sara, go through the motions. Put a smile on, stand up tall, and be strong. Don't let anyone down.* My parents looked like children in a candy store, with their bright smiling faces and cheerful voices.

"Sara, look at the view from here. You can sit outside and have a picnic," my mom squealed. "This is amazing. Look at this campus," said my dad.

I smiled and nodded and thought to myself, *at least someone is happy.* I thought when I got to Whittier my eating disorder would magically disappear. But that did not happen. If anything, I felt worse. *Oh, shit, Sara.* I had been relying on that quick fix.

"Next in line!" I looked up and one of the RAs was waving me over to her station. We walked over to the table. "Name please?" she asked. "Sara Gottfried," I said. "While I'm finding your student ID, let me give you some information for today. You will move through each of the next few tables, in which you will receive materials and directions on moving into your dorm. Tonight there will be a freshman orientation ceremony that families are invited to. It is somewhat of a sendoff and a fun way to celebrate move-in day. There are plenty of people here to help you move in should you need help or have any other questions. Here is your student ID card, and welcome to Whittier College!"

I took my ID and, without any time to think or even respond, we were directed to the next table. By the end, I had no hands left. I was given a plethora of Whittier College gear, a drawstring bag, lanyard, and pen, to name a few, in addition to various textbooks and folders of information. My parents and I made our way back to the car to begin the actual move-in process. My dad drove the car around campus to my room, where we hauled bags and bags of clothes, bedding, and office supplies into my dorm. It was hot as hell that day, sweat dripping from all the wrong places.

My roommate was out at the time I moved in, so it was just my parents and me. I set up my pictures above the bed, but the humidity was so sticky, the Command Strips would not hold. My dad did the manly things; he set up the printer, connected the ethernet cables, and finished carrying in all the heavy boxes. My mom and I, well, we did the domestic things—we decorated and organized and then did some more decorating and organizing. At any moment of pause, my mind resorted to anxiety. *You cannot do this. This will not work out. What am I going to do when Mom and Dad leave? What happens if I get anxious and my mom is not here? What happens if I cannot eat? What happens if I do not like the food? What happens if I want to leave and go home?* As these thoughts interspersed throughout my mind, I kept telling myself to just go through the motions. *Keep organizing, Sara. Keep smiling, Sara. Keep looking happy.*

After a few hours, my roommate and her parents walked in. My roommate was tall with brown hair. Just by looking at her, I knew she was down to earth and warm. Her side of the room was clean and organized, and that says a lot about someone, especially a college roommate. My first impression of Kaitlyn was that we would get along. We had already been texting in the weeks leading up to move-in day, and we seemed to click.

Kaitlyn and her parents stood by the door as my parents, and I stood by my bed. No one knew what to say or how to say it. Do we hug or do we shake hands? Do we introduce ourselves first or should we let them go first? Everyone looked at each other with haphazard smiles. I felt my inner child come out as I quickly glanced at my parents, insinuating them to make the first move. And when they did not, I put my big girl panties on. Kaitlyn did the same, and we moved toward one another to shake hands. It felt so formal. I think we both wanted to give one another a hug but it was a moment of, *Wait, we do not really know each other that well so let's start with a handshake.* You could feel the awkwardness in the room begin to dissipate because soon I was shaking hands with Kaitlyn's parents just as she was doing the same with my parents. We engaged in small talk, which is my least favorite kind of talk however fitting for the situation.

The conversation only lasted ten minutes or so and then Kaitlyn's parents began their departure, which prompted my parents to begin theirs, which only exacerbated my anxiety. Of course, my parents had to leave. They were not the ones going to college. They had to go home. They had work. They had a life. But I wanted, no I *deserved*, a proper goodbye. I wanted some time to sit with them, hug them, and talk to them. Instead, my parents chose to say goodbye in front of my roommate and her parents. And by goodbye, my dad said, "All right, Sara, we are going to get going. Give us a hug." My dad put his arms around me, or all that was left of me. My bones protruded through my shirt. It was a light hug. My dad was not a big touchy-feely guy, but I also think he was so afraid of hugging me, so afraid that even the lightest squeeze might break me, literally. He kissed me on the head and backed away as my mom came in for a hug. Her hug was tighter, but it was shorter. She caressed her hand against my back during the hug. My dad gave me one last pat against the shoulder, and that was it. My mom grabbed her purse and they left, waving goodbye, smiles on their faces.

Maybe a quick goodbye was what I needed in that moment. I needed to continue going through the motions because if I took a moment to feel, that would have welcomed all hell to break loose. Instead of fighting back, I went with it. I was going to see them in a few hours at the sendoff ceremony, but I was only going to see them in the distance; I was not actually going to get to spend more time with them.

For the remainder of the afternoon, my roommate Kaitlyn and I met up with some other classmates. There was a Whittier College Class of 2019 Facebook group that everyone joined upon receiving their acceptance letter. That was how Kaitlyn and I had met and how we befriended some other people. I met a girl named Danielle in the group. She was from Portland,

Maine, and we met up twice in Boston over the summer. Danielle was sensible and humorous. She knew how to have fun and when to turn it off. As she spoke, the excitement in her voice took over. Her face was full of joy and her heart-shaped lips created her sweet and innocent presence. She was also a yogi, so we naturally connected.

Danielle's roommate, Samantha, also sat with us. Samantha was from Seattle, Washington. Her sand-colored hair accentuated her thin face and bright blue eyes. Her pearly white teeth finished her charming look. Samantha carried a confidence that shined through as she spoke. She had an air about her that made you feel like you were in the "cool" group. We all sat down on couches and talked.

Samantha: "There is a party one night this week. We should totally go." "We definitely should!" Danielle cheerfully said. "How do you think classes are going to be tomorrow? Have you guys picked up your books yet?" Kaitlyn asked. "Not yet. I need to do that tomorrow," said Danielle. "Same," said Samantha.

As we—or should I say *they*—talked, the realization that my parents were leaving that night began to set in more concretely. Physically, I was sitting with the girls on the couch, but mentally, I was lost in my thoughts, hyper focused on what the fuck I had gotten myself in to and how the fuck I was going to make it through today, let alone the next four years. I attempted to talk myself out of it, focusing on the conversation. For a moment I was able to regroup and become present. In some ways I had to; we were heading to the dining hall, and my mind was only equipped to handle one thing at a time. It had to have enough free space to handle food, especially food in a college dining hall. We walked halfway across campus, which felt like a million miles, through the sweltering and hazy heat. Kaitlyn and I walked off to the right to find our table. Freshmen quickly started to shuffle in like dogs when they hear the deli drawer open in the refrigerator. *Food, give me some! Get into my belly, now!* Dining hall staff served us plates of coconut chicken and rice. It looked appetizing and it smelled sweet. I picked up my knife and fork and cut the chicken into pieces. Without hesitation, I stabbed a piece of chicken onto the fork and opened my mouth. This was a new moment for me. Usually, I spent a great deal of time cutting up my food, separating it out on the plate, and chewing each bite ever so slowly as though I'm a toddler trying spinach for the first time. Something inside me told me to just go for it. *Eat the food, Sara.* Everyone else is eating and you need to fit in.

As I chewed the chicken, one bite after another, I wrestled the coconut out of my teeth. The chicken was good. I did not finish the whole plate. That was not allowed in my rule book. Instead, I left half of the chicken and three-quarters of the rice on the plate.

I was hungry enough that I allowed myself to eat such a foreign meal but could not fathom being a part of the clean plate club. When I finished, I looked around. Everyone else was eating. It was amazing. No one looked like they had any disordered eating. They were all just eating and talking, less focused on the food and more focused on the conversation. It was refreshing. I noticed that some people chose the vegetarian option, which had a lot more vegetables. There was a moment I wondered if I should have opted for that instead. I checked in with myself. I was clear. My anxiety had subsided. *Sara, you are okay.*

After dinner, we walked outside, making our way to the outdoor stage, where the ceremony was taking place. There were so many people. So much noise. The stimulation was overwhelming. The anxiety began to set back in. Would I see my parents before they officially left? How am I going to get through this? I don't know what to do. The panic began to intensify. *No, please heart, slow down. Don't do this to me. I can't do this. I can't do this. I can't do this. I need my mom.* It was too late to do anything now; we were already heading to our seats. Everyone around me was smiling, except for me. Once we took our seats, I located my parents in the distance. I took out my phone and texted my mom: *I can't do this. I don't want to do this. I was just saying I wanted this to see if it would make me better.*

Bing.

What are you talking about? my mom responded. *I can't do this. I will kill myself if I stay here. I can't do this.* *Bing.* *Put your phone down. This is ridiculous. You said you wanted this. You've been talking about this for months.* I didn't put my phone down. I kept repeating the same thing: *I can't do this. I don't want to be here.* I wasn't paying attention to what was going on or what the presenters were saying, and before I knew it, the ceremony was over. As everyone stood up, I walked over to my parents. The walk felt long and treacherous, as though I were running a marathon, just about to cross the finish line, so close yet so far.

"Sara, what are you doing? You're supposed to be over there with your class," my mom said. "I don't know. I can't do this," I said. As I moved toward my mom, hoping for a hug, she moved away. "What do you mean you can't do this? I'm not doing this right now. This is what you want. This is what you have told us you want. Go back in line," my mom growled.

I did not go back in line. Instead, I stared at her, locking my eyes onto hers. My dad, a rocket ready to explode, turned to my mom and said, "Is she kidding us right now?" "I don't know Michael. I'm not doing this," said my mom.

None of us said anything. We all looked at each other with fear, hate, and anger in our eyes. Fear of what it meant if I did not stay. Hate for my terrible fucking eating disorder. And anger, well, that was the only emotion my dad really knew. "Come over here, Sara. Sit down," said my mom.

That is what my mom does. She is a peacemaker, a people pleaser. When she feels the tension between my dad and I rise, she intervenes and tries to problem solve in the most convoluted of ways, even when she herself feels anger and hatred. We sat down on a bench. My dad just stared at me. "Sara, what is going on? This is what you have wanted for so long. You have been talking about this for the past year. Where is this coming from?" my mom asked.

For the last year, I lied. I lied to my family. I lied to Julie, my nutritionist, and Erin, my therapist. But most of all, I lied to myself. I thought that if I went over 3,000 miles across the country, some miracle would befall me. I thought I would be free from my eating disorder. I thought a new environment, away from the toxicity of my family and friends, would somehow shake me out of my eating disorder. But that did not happen. It was all too much. I was not strong enough mentally, emotionally, or physically to handle college, let alone college across the country.

I looked at my mom. "I don't know. I just can't do this. Can I stay with you guys tonight at the hotel? I know another girl who is staying with her parents at the hotel for a few nights until classes start. Can I do that, too?" "Sara, you are all moved in. What are you going to say to Kaitlyn?"

Here we go, again. It's always about what other people think. It's always about playing house and making it look like everything is dandy. "She's not going to say anything. No one is. No one is going to care. Other people are doing it so I don't understand why I can't." I could see my mom's chest expand as she inhaled a deep breath. "Whatever." The conversation went in circles for the next hour. It went from *Sara, you need to do this,* to staring at one another, back to *I can't do this.*

After an hour, my anxiety subsided. That's the thing about anxiety—it's really hard to tell when it will pass. Yeah, sure there are breathing techniques, Cognitive-Behavioral Therapy interventions, and a myriad of other coping skills, but in that exact moment when you are plagued— no, *paralyzed* with anxiety—there is no way of getting out of it. The only way out is through. Literally, you have to ride the waves. For me, I can feel when my anxiety has passed. My face feels cooler, my heartbeat becomes more rhythmic, my mind becomes clearer, and I feel present. I looked at my mom and said, "Okay." She looked at me kind of like how a mother looks at a young child who has just fallen off his bike and scraped his knee. "You are okay honey. You will be okay." We hugged and kissed again. We parted ways again. That night I fell right to sleep. Anxiety knocks the wind out of you. Sleep is the only way to recover.

The next morning, it started all over again. The anxiety set in. I felt my heart drop toward my feet. My body felt heavy and warm. My mind went crazy. *You will kill yourself if you stay here, Sara. You cannot do this. Get out of here, fast.* I tried to work through it. I went to breakfast. I did not eat. I could not eat. Like I said, my mind was only equipped to handle one thing at a time, and at that moment its only goal was to get the fuck out of there. After breakfast, somehow, I went to my first class. I watched the clock for the entire ninety-minutes. I do not remember what even happened during that class because my mind was so preoccupied with texting my mom. I continued to repeat the same things over and over again: *I can't do this. I will kill myself. I'm not staying here.*

Get help. This is ridiculous. You need to go to the counseling center. You need to get help, my mom responded. When the class was over, I picked up my backpack and raced out of the classroom. Each step I took I felt my body become weaker, my legs twigs in the grass. I could not help but wonder if this would be my last step. My mind and body, who had been at war with one another for the last two years, felt about to both give out, neither able to win. I could see the counseling center in the distance, atop the hill, but I was unsure how I would get there. *Sara, keep going. One foot in front of the other. Deep breath in, deep breath out.*

I made it. Thank God! I walked up the ramp and opened the door. A woman greeted me. She was warm and friendly. Tears streamed down my face. I did not even try to wipe them away. "Is everything okay?" she asked.

"I have an eating disorder. I can't do this. I want to go home." It was the first time I ever came out, without hesitation, and stated I had an eating disorder. I was desperate, in survival mode, so I would say anything to anyone if it meant I could potentially be saved.

"Okay. Let me get one of our counselors. Hang tight for a moment," she said. A few minutes later a middle-aged gentleman walked over to me. "Sara, would you like to come into my office?" My feet moved faster than my mouth. I followed him through a hallway into a room. He turned to me and said, "What has been going on?"

My recollection of this day is unclear. I know I told him I had an eating disorder and that I wanted to go home, but I do not remember the specific questions he asked or how I answered. What I do remember is the most important question any mental health professional ever asks, which is, "Are you going to hurt yourself?"

Now before I get into how I responded, let me explain something first. This question is twofold. Yes, mental health professionals are mandated reporters, so if a client says, "Yes, I am going to hurt myself," they are mandated to get you help, or rather, send you to the hospital. But if you answer *yes*, they listen, like *actually listen* to you. So, was I going to hurt myself? I do not know. Probably not. I did not have a plan nor the means, but I did have all the reasons why killing myself was a viable and necessary option. Like I said, I was in survival mode. I was willing to do anything and everything to get the hell out of college.

So, when he looked at me and asked, "Are you going to hurt yourself?" I, without a doubt, said, "Yes, I will," because that was his cue to listen and take what I was saying seriously. That was what I needed to convince my parents that taking me home was the right thing to do. If my parents were not going to take me seriously, then this knucklehead sure would after my response. There was a moment of silence and then he just looked at me and said, "I think we need to call your parents." Before I could respond, he got up and walked out of the office. I sat there, staring off.

Panic started to set in again. It was not panic stemming from my anxiety, it was panic of what my parents were going to think, what they would say. I didn't have much time to think on this because the counselor walked back in the room and thirty-minutes later, my parents arrived from the hotel down the street.

My mom walked in first. Her face was white and shiny. It was hot and humid that day, the sweat was visible between her eyelids. She looked sick herself. Her body exhausted from everything I—no, *we*—had been through. She barely made eye contact with me. My dad followed behind. He left a trail of anger as he sat down. The psychologist looked at my parents and I and said, "There are options. Sara could go to a program, get some help, and then slowly transition back to school. We can help her throughout this process." My mom shook her head in disbelief.

My dad, hands crossed looking stoic, cut the counselor off mid-sentence and said, "This is ridiculous." My mom looked at me and said, "Let's go then. If this is what you want, then go pack up your stuff and let's go." As mad, frustrated, and confused as my parents were and as much as that scared me, I felt a wave of relief come over me. My mind felt clearer. My heartbeat slowed down to a normal pace. I knew I made the right decision. I had no resentment. I felt free. I was content. Although I did not know how I was going to make it through at home or what my relationship would now be like with my parents or even what people back home would think, I was okay with this unknowing. That day I marched myself into the counseling office, that day I said *I can't do this*, was the first day of the rest of my life.

The counselor looked at us and said, "Okay." He told us the first thing we should do is retrieve all my things from my dorm and that we can deal with admissions and the financial aid office when I got home. So, that's just what we did. We walked back to my dorm room, and we packed up my stuff. No one talked. Silence speaks louder than words. No one even looked at one another. The air was thick. You could feel the tension permeate the room. We packed up what we could, which included clothes, pictures, and electronics. Everything else, we left. No one knew I was leaving. Everyone was in class.

As we drove off, I texted Kaitlyn and Danielle and told them I was leaving. They felt bad, obviously. But we had only known one another for a very short period. What could they say? The decision had already been made. I was going home. When we arrived at the hotel, the first thing my dad said to me was, "Sara, I don't even know if there are any seats left on the plane. You are going to pay for this ticket."

Typical for my dad to be focused solely on money. It was also typical for him to revert his attention to anything but emotions. My mom said, "Sara, I don't even know what you are going to do when you get home. Julie and Erin might not want to see you again. They are not going to trust you. You are going to need to work and get a job. You cannot live like this. You need to get help. Dad and I cannot help you anymore."

I did not respond. Instead, I took a deep breath in and let a deep breath out. *Sara, it is okay. You are going home. Everything is going to be okay.* We all beat to our own drum for the rest of the afternoon. My mom sat on the deck attached to our hotel room. My dad retreated within himself and sat in the concierge lounge. I laid on the bed, staring at the ceiling. A million thoughts raced through my mind: What am I going to do when I get home? What if Julie and Erin don't want to see me? Who will help me now? I don't have any friends. They said I need to get a job. I could be a nanny. It was so typical of me to make a plan for anything other than how I was going to overcome my eating disorder because I truly did not know how I was going to recover.

I looked over at my mom sitting outside on the deck, legs crossed. I got off the bed and walked outside. I sat down on the couch next to her. "Can we talk?" I asked. I do not remember the conversation all that well. At that point, it was late in the day. I was exhausted. So much had happened. So much had been said. It was hard to even think straight. My mom just looked at me, blank-faced. It was the first time in a long time she was completely speechless. A problem avoider at heart, my mom did not have the answer. I looked into her eyes and said, "I'm sorry." I was all cried out. I had no tears left to shed. She just looked at me. "I know you are, Sara. I know. I don't know what you are going to do. This was what you wanted." "I will pay for the plane ticket. I will pay you guys back," I said. "Sara, this has nothing to do with money. That's not even on my radar. You need to get help." I nodded. "I know," I said.

I pulled my phone out of my pocket and texted my grandmother. *Can I stay over tomorrow night when we get back?*

My mom went back in the hotel room as I waited for a response from my grandmother. I thought about what things would be like now. Would I need to move in with my grandmother? Would I need to live with her? Would she be my new mom?

Ring!

I looked at my phone and my grandmother's name appeared. She was calling me. I put the phone to my ear and said hello.

"Hi, Sara, it's me, Grandma. How are you doing? What is going on?"

Her voice was not as empathetic and nurturing as I thought it would be. I am not sure if she just did not know how to respond to everything that was going on or she felt an alliance toward my mom who had already informed her of what was going on.

"I don't know. I just can't do this. I don't really want to talk about it. Can I stay over tomorrow night? I think it would be best."

"I understand, honey. You can stay over. Let me know what you want for dinner, and I will make it. I love you."

"I love you," I said.

That was the first time I said *I love you* to my grandmother in over two years. The words just kind of slipped out of my mouth. I am not quite sure if I said it because I truly meant it or if I said it because it was the right thing to do. Either way, the words came out and I could not take them back. What was said had been said. At least I had a place to stay tomorrow, I thought.

The next day, we boarded the plane and went home. Silence continued to permeate the air around us. No one said a word on the drive to the airport, on the plane ride, or even on the drive back home. As my dad put his blinker on and turned into our neighborhood, a wave of sadness came over me. It was not an emotion I had felt in a while. I was so accustomed to anxiety and frustration that sadness had no room in my life. But as we drove down the street and pulled up the driveway, I could not help but wonder what my life had in store. I thought the hardest part was saying I wanted to go home. But the hardest part would be truly beating this eating disorder, which included the physical act of eating. When we walked in the door, everything was as we left it. The dish towel was perfectly hung up on the oven. The blanket was folded and set in its basket. Not a speck of dust on the floor. We each set our suitcases on the floor in the living room. Before my parents started to unpack, I looked at them and said, "I am going to sleep at grandma's tonight. I think it is best for me."

My dad looked at me and did not say anything. My mom just said, "Okay."

I packed my bag and left. We needed space from one another. We all needed time to think. When I got to my grandmother's house and opened the door, she walked over to me, put her arms out, and embraced me. She hugged me tight. I could smell the crisp smoke within her clothes. As she released me, she took the bag from my hand and guided me into the living room. We sat down and I burrowed my face between her breasts as she wrapped her arms around me. She rested her chin on top of my head. We sat in silence and hugged. This was new for us. This whole hugging and being vulnerable thing.

After a few minutes, I sat upright and stared off in the distance. What was I doing here? I needed to be home. I just spent the past three days—actually, the past two *years*—battling myself, and after finally realizing I needed to be home, I was still not at home. I was still doing anything and everything to avoid the very place that would heal me. Maybe unconsciously I knew that home was where I needed to be to recover, but the act of recovering was so scary. Home was where I was going recover. And more importantly, home was where I was going to be reborn. "Sara, would you like some dinner?" my grandmother asked, snapping me out of my gaze. I looked at my grandmother and said, "I think I'm going to go home. I think home is where I need to be right now." My grandmother looked at me and gave me a hug. "Sara, I think that is a good idea. If you need anything tonight, call me. I love you."

When I arrived home shortly after, my parents were sitting on the couch. My mom looked over at me and asked, "Sara, what are you doing home? I thought you were staying over at Grandma's." "I was going to, but I think it's best if I'm home right now. Is it okay that I'm here?" "Yes, that's fine. Of course, it is."

My parents did not say much. We were all exhausted. We had nothing left to say to one another. It had been a long day and we all needed rest.

That night, I laid in my bed looking at the ceiling as though it was a bright blue sky. I imagined the bird again, the one I saw when I was at the hotel the morning of move-in day. I saw him soaring through the sky alone. He had a broken wing, but he kept going, kept flying on. With the summer upon him, he flew back home. He snuggled into his mother's wings and slept. After a few short days, his wing healed. Birds fly all around the world. They migrate to warmer places in the cooler months, but they always go back home. And I too, had finally gone back home. Back home to heal, just like the bird. Back home to live, just like the bird.

October 2015

The next month was challenging. It was the first time I *really* went into battle with my eating disorder. It was now or never. I had a support team, but most importantly I had the support of myself, which perhaps was the missing piece all along. As cliché as the saying is, until I admitted I had a problem, I was not ready to get better. I hit rock bottom when I was at Whittier College. I had two paths in that moment. I could veer left and go down a sickening and deathly track, full of anger, depression, and ultimately suicide, or I could make one of the hardest decisions of my life and veer right onto the path of recovery.

I met with Julie weekly when I returned home. I remember opening the door to her studio, everything in its same place just as we left off. The cubbies were still to the left when you walked in. The white Ikea desk with a bucket of barre socks sitting on top and the coat rack hanging on the opposite wall of the cubbies. Julie she greeted me the same way she greeted me when I first met her. She opened her arms and gave me a hug. She did not greet me with an energetic smile, but instead greeted me with warmth and empathy. Her physical embrace was tangible and rooted. Her hands pressed into my shoulder blades. Her hair wisped about my face. And as she stepped back, her hands still sitting atop my shoulders, she looked at me in the eyes and said, "It's going to be okay." In that moment, I felt like Julie was my fairy godmother sent from the heavens above. In reality, she was not. She was my nutritionist. But she welcomed be back with open arms, literally and figuratively.

We walked into the yoga studio and sat on bolsters. "How are you feeling?" Julie asked. "Okay," I responded. "I'm going to be honest with you. I had a feeling college was going to be difficult." I looked down at my hands. "I'm here to help you, and I'm going to push you harder this time around. You can do this. Okay?" "Okay," I said.

Julie started where we left off, but this time around was different. I was not doing it for anyone else, I was doing it for myself. Up until this point, I did not realize that I could use my qualities of rigidity, persistence, and drive—the ones that got me into this very eating disorder—to overcome it. Persistence got me through each food challenge. Rigidity allowed me to follow Julie's guidelines to a *T*. And, drive, well, that got me to where I finally ended up... in recovery.

My body had been malnourished for almost three years, and it was deteriorating more by the day. The amount of food I needed just to simply refuel my body was unfathomable, let alone the amount of food I needed to gain weight.

When I left Whittier College, I made a pledge that I was going to eat, that I was not going to kill myself, and that I was not going to die from this fucking disorder.

As I said, before I could even begin to gain weight, I needed to maintain my current weight. Unfortunately, or maybe fortunately, I did not know my weight. I had not known my weight for the past two years. What I did know is that I needed a significant number of daily calories to stay at my current weight, around the ballpark of 3,500. Julie put me on a strict food regimen. I did not have the flexibility to be choosy with my foods. I did what she told me to do over the next eight months. I didn't log my food intake during this time, and unlike Tara and the hospital, there were no rigid and strict meal plans. Of course, Julie had guidelines she wanted me to follow, such as ensuring I was eating three meals a day, in addition to two or three daily snacks. Julie knew if I was being honest about what I was eating as the number on the scale doesn't lie. This time around, however, I felt pain when I lost weight or even when I maintained my weight. I did not want to die anymore. I wanted to keep saving myself and my body. I wanted to win. I was no longer in a place in which losing weight and seeing doctors' faces go numb created a sense of enjoyment and satisfaction. Instead, seeing Julie's face when I lost weight or maintained my weight made me feel defeated and sad.

Around the eight-month mark, I began to reach what they call "weight restoration." Weight restoration is the process in eating disorder recovery when the person reaches a "healthy" weight. Now, "healthy" is ambiguous because of the Body Positivity movement and the Health at Every Size philosophy that believes there is a continuum for being at a healthy weight, which can range drastically. There are also a variety of indicators for reaching a healthy weight, aside from solely a scale. For Julie, at the time, weight restoration included the number on the scale and my overall appearance, physically and mentally. I reached a place where I could fit into clothes and go shopping at stores. I could go out to dinner, although some internal rules still existed. But perhaps the two biggest indicators included going back to school and exercising again. I did not reach weight restoration overnight. Some might say it took me years, others may say it took me only eight months. Just like getting into an eating disorder, getting out is not a linear process. I did not consistently gain weight at each appointment or even maintain. There were times I lost weight, whether that be an ounce or a few pounds. There were days and even weeks when I felt like giving up. Throwing in the towel seemed easier. But the only way out of something is through it. And that's just what I did.

As for my parents, there was no magic pill that led us to becoming a cohesive unit again. We did not engage in some grand family therapy session that allowed us to release our anger, frustration, and anxiety. In fact, there was not much talking about my eating disorder. My parents had done what they could to help me. Instead, they assumed their positions. When we returned home, my mom returned to work and my dad began travelling again. I got a job at an after-school program in my town, working a few hours in the morning and afternoon Monday through Friday. Work gave us all individual time, time to be away from one another. But family dinners started to return to normal and represent a time for us to all come together and laugh, catch up on with one another and just be. It took time for things to go back to normal. Just like I didn't get better overnight, neither did my relationship with my parents. But as I got better physically, my mental and emotional health followed in suit. I had the brain width to take on more, to focus on my relationships that had deteriorated over the last few years. I was able to see the bigger picture. I was more in tune with reality. And with all of this, I slowly began to find myself again, the Sara that had been buried underneath pain and hurt for so long. She began to resurface. This Sara was brighter, more determined, and more importantly, resilient.

January 2016

After four months of hard work and dedication, I started a new journey. One of the biggest indicators of my weight restoration was my ability to go to college and stay there.

I was a A-/B+ student in high school. I took mostly honors courses and was a stickler for completing my homework immediately upon walking in the door after school. Even throughout my eating disorder, nights where I was having panic attacks over too much oil being in the pan or afraid to take even the smallest bite of peanut butter, my work ethic never changed. It was the only thing that was a constant. It was my only focus, other than my eating disorder. College was something I had looked forward to since middle school. I had dreams of going to an amazing college.

As I made my way through high school, my top choice schools became more realistic. Maybe I was not going to get into an Ivy League school, but maybe I could get into a prestigious liberal arts school, like Whittier College, or a known Boston college, like Simmons University. Like many rising high school students, there are schools deemed "not good enough." I had not want to go to school near my parents. I had not wanted to go to a school that *everyone* goes to. I wanted to go somewhere different, somewhere new. And although I tried, it did not work. The reason I say all of this is because I ended up at the very college I never thought I'd step foot in. But for me, that school was the very place I needed to be.

January of 2016 marked the start of my undergraduate career at Bridgewater State University, where I intended to major in Social Work. I remember my first day vividly. I commuted to campus, and despite the campus being spread out, I found ease getting around. I scoped out the campus beforehand and practiced my route in preparation for my first day. It was a relief knowing that I did not need to conquer an entire campus. Instead, I only needed to get acclimated to one building at a time. My classes were in one of two buildings, and that was a relief. The building that housed both the library and academic classrooms was old and had a musty smell when you walked in. The doors made a loud creaking sound when they opened, and the elevators were so small, the anticipation of potentially getting stuck was enough to make you avoid taking it at all costs. The library was on the third floor and the classrooms were on the first and second.

The other building, which housed my social work classes, was newer. The lights were brighter, compared to the dim yellow lights of the library. I always felt myself become a little more present when I walked into the building. The feeling was similar to when I was in high school and sick in my eating disorder, and I craved the moment the clock hit 1:49 p.m. so that I could go home. The moment I walked into my house and now when I walked into the social work building brought a sense of relief. *Sara, you are home.* The building had three floors, but classes were located on the first floor and professors' offices were located on the second and third floors. There was a large common area with cafeteria-style tables in the middle. Unlike in high school and even middle school, sitting alone at a table did not deem you uncool. Everyone was in their own world pursuing their education because they wanted to be there.

My classes were small. My professors were insightful, most of them holding their doctorates. Bridgewater State University was everything I had been looking for in my original college search. It's funny how the world works sometimes.

I started off taking three classes to ease into things. I was still working on recovery, and I was still working at the after-school program. I did not want to overwhelm myself right off the bat. I got into a routine like I always do. On Mondays and Wednesdays, I woke up around 6:30 a.m. and drove to school, arriving at 7:30 a.m. I sat at the same table in the common area, eating my yogurt parfait. At 7:50 a.m., I went to my 8 a.m. class, Introduction to Sociology, followed by my 9:30 a.m. class, First Year Seminar: Food, Feast, and Folly. At 10:45 a.m., I drove home, studied, ate lunch, and did some more studying until 2:30 p.m. when I headed to work until 6p.m. On Tuesdays and Thursdays, I had a similar routine. I woke up at the same time and drove to campus for my 8a.m. class, Writing Rhetorically with Sources. I usually stayed in the library for a few hours until noon to study and do homework until I headed home around 1p.m. for work. I had off Fridays from classes.

That became my weekly routine, and I thrived.

March 2016

School was not the only indicator of my getting better. Exercise was, too. Every week, I took Bill's Saturday morning Weekend Warrior class. His beginner's yoga class was one of my initial introductions to yoga, and now I had progressed to a faster and heated yoga class. It was equal parts movement and stillness. The movement sparked empowerment, vitality, and confidence, as I inhaled into Star Pose and exhaled into Warrior II. Tree Pose evoked stability and strength, as I balanced on one leg, hands at heart center. The stillness of Child's Pose brought me peace and restoration, while Savasana tested my ability to engage in stillness. Yoga awakened my soul. I felt powerful. For so long, movement had been deemed "bad," the ultimate antagonist against my recovery. But in fact, yoga was my saving grace. When I was working with the doctors at the hospital and even with Tara, I was not allowed to exercise. The gym was equivalent to death, literally and metaphorically.

When I met Julie, exercise was not deemed "bad," but it was deemed secondary. If I was eating, then I could practice yoga. However, Julie knew I was going to practice whether I ate or not, whether I lost weight or gained weight, or whether I truly wanted to exercise. Why implement rules and regulations that she knew I was not going to follow? So many medical professionals preach exercise should not be a part of eating disorder recovery even though most sufferers engage in exercise anyway. Why not implement healthy and adaptive forms of exercise into recovery to bridge that gap, to meet the patient where they are at? This is not to condone drastic forms of exercise, but it is to allow for a sense of normality. Julie knew this. Julie accepted this. And most importantly, Julie worked this into my plan.

When I first started yoga two years previous, I was only a junior in high school, getting sicker by the day. Laura opened the door. The hospital closed that door almost immediately. When I took Bill's beginner's yoga class, he opened that door back up for me. Now, almost a year later, that door remained open because Julie never closed it. Although yoga did not cure me, it complimented my recovery. It was safe. It allowed my body the ability to move freely and safely. It allowed my soul to shine. And it allowed my mind to remain present. So, it was not a surprise when Universal Power Yoga sent an email announcing an upcoming Kids Yoga Teacher Training with Kim Taylor of Cardio Kids Yoga that I was eager to sign up. At my next appointment with Julie, I sat down with her and talked through the training. Julie was both a yoga and barre instructor and knew many people in the business. She said I was a perfect for the training, so I signed up.

Kim Taylor is a life changer. She is a wave of love. Her eyes are big and inviting. When she walks in the room, the energy changes. You can feel her warmth and light. She teaches with intelligence, experience, and passion. When I took the Kids Yoga Teacher Training with Kim, my life was forever changed. She reaffirmed my love for learning, for teaching, and most importantly, for putting those two passions together to make the world a better place for children. Kim taught me the fundamentals of teaching kids' yoga and of creating a business. When I graduated her weekend training, I felt more confident in myself. I kickstarted my own business, Stretch Yourself Yoga: Stretching your limits mentally, emotionally, and physically. I embarked on yet another journey, in which I became Sara the businessperson and children's yoga teacher. I cold called businesses, taught free classes, and created partnerships and collaborated with charities. I developed a personal website and marketing campaign. I was moving forward. My purpose in this world was becoming more succinct and tangible. I was thriving, mentally, emotionally, and physically.

June 2016

Life was continuing to get better. I finished my spring classes, but that did not stop me from playing catchup. I took five classes over the summer so that I was on track to graduate. I worked at a summer camp Monday through Friday, and I continued to make my mark in the world of kid's yoga. Life was good. Actually, life was great. The two biggest indicators of my recovery included going to college and exercising. But perhaps the most significant indicator was when I stopped seeing Julie. That summer, I reached a point of weight restoration. I was able to enjoy the daily acts of human life, although some rules still existed.

How did I get here? Why did I get here? So many people die from this ugly disorder, but what did I do to deserve to live through this? These are questions I continue to ask myself. Maybe it my personality that equipped me with the right ingredients to fight and survive. Maybe it was a privilege that my parents had good insurance and could afford to get me the care I needed. Was it luck that I found Julie? I do not know what the answer is. Maybe it is a combination of things. Or maybe, just maybe, it was me. Throughout this whole obstacle course, I still had dreams. My body was slowing giving out, but my mind never gave up. Despite my inability to eat, I still imagined myself living across the country, going to school, becoming a social worker, and teaching yoga. I chose to get better. Yes, I had all the right "ingredients." And yes, I was fortunate enough to come from a financially-stable family, but I chose to get better. I made the most difficult decision I will probably ever have to make. I chose to live. No one can do that for you. Only you can. Only I could do that for myself. And that's just what I did. My decision is what saved me. My recovery is because of me and no one else.

I saved myself.

ACKNOWLEDGMENTS

My memoir is a culmination of four years of dedication, passion, and trust. I am eternally grateful for my tribe and the endless support they have shown me throughout my journey.

I want to first acknowledge, Julie Starr, the epitome of compassion and patience. I consider Julie Starr my saving grace. I truly do not know where I would be today had I not met her nine years ago. Since day one, Julie has treated me like a person, not a patient. She has guided me every step of the way, continuously showing up for me through the most challenging of days. I am forever grateful for Julie. She has and always will have such a special place in my heart.

To Christine Meade, my editor, the one who has been my partner throughout the writing process. Christine has not only been my editor, but she has been my truth seeker, helping me to craft my memoir. Christine never saw me as the young girl I was in my story. She has always looked at me as a writer, with so much potential and passion.

My mom and dad, my parents, who have stayed along for the ride. This book is not only a memoir of my life, but a story of our family and what we have overcome. Our experiences and challenges have only made us stronger. Thank you for supporting me in helping my memoir come to fruition and always reminding me that anything I set my mind to I can and will accomplish.

To Mike, my partner, a man I never thought existed. For being my number one supporter throughout this process and reminding me of the importance of sharing my story. Time and time again, you have shown me that I am so much more than my physical body. Words cannot describe how thankful I am to have you in my life.

Finally, to all those who have been a part of my journey: Kristie Gillooly my soulful photographer; Chantelle Davis and Ashley Mason, my web designer and social media partners in crime.

Thank you for being part of my journey and helping me to tell my truth.

Love,
Sara

AUTHOR BIO

Sara Gottfried graduated from Bridgewater State University with a Bachelor of Science degree and went on to complete an Advanced Standing Social Work program at Boston University, obtaining her Master of Social Work.

Sara is a Licensed Clinical Social Worker (LCSW) in Massachusetts. She works as a School Social Worker at a school outside of Boston and as a therapist at a private practice. Sara is also a member of the National Association of Social Workers Massachusetts Chapter and dedicates her time volunteering with the organization.

When not working as a social worker or writing, Sara can be found hiking throughout New England, exploring coffee shops, or traveling.

Full: A Memoir of Overcoming an Eating Disorder is her first memoir.

Printed in Great Britain
by Amazon

38928167R00108